SECRET GLOUCESTER

Christine Jordan

To my mum who was an enigma, and to my dad who is a fighter.

First published 2015

Amberley Publishing
The Hill, Stroud
Gloucestershire, GL5 4EP

www.amberley-books.com

ISBN 978 1 4456 4688 6 (print)
ISBN 978 1 4456 4689 3 (ebook)

British Library Cataloguing in Publication Data.
A catalogue record for this book is available from the British Library.

Typesetting by Amberley Publishing.
Printed in Great Britain.

Contents

	Introduction	4
1	Historic Gloucester	9
2	Religious Gloucester	34
3	Industrial Gloucester	47
4	Military Gloucester	59
5	Notable Gloucestrians	66
6	Treasures of Gloucester	74
7	Musical Gloucester	85
8	Epicurean Gloucester	91
	About the Author	95
	Acknowledgements	96

Introduction

'As sure as God's in Gloucester.'

This medieval proverb was in common use throughout the Middle Ages and well into the seventeenth century before falling into disuse.

William Malmesbury (1095–1143), one of the foremost chroniclers of his time, claimed the saying arose because of 'the fruitfulness of it [Gloucester] in Religion' in that it is said to have 'returned the Seed of the Gospel with the Increase of an hundred Fold'. Thomas Cromwell (1485–1540) remarked, when he visited the city, that it had 'more churches than Godliness!' It seems that little had changed of visitors' opinions of the city when later, Thomas Fuller (1608–1661) said the proverb originated 'on account that there were more rich and mitred Abbeys in Gloucester than in any two shires' but he added that the saying was 'no more fit to be used than a toad is wholesome to be eaten.' The Godliness, or otherwise, of Gloucester remains a matter of opinion!

It's easy to see how this saying came into being when you consider the many religious houses that sprang up in Gloucester from the founding of St Peter's Abbey, now Gloucester Cathedral, in AD 678 to the many parochial churches scattered about the city. Whatever the opinion of visitors to the city today, there is no doubting that it still possesses an inordinate number of religious buildings. Some have been demolished, built over or become places of historical interest and, in some cases, tourist attractions.

Culture and civilisation have been almost continuous in Gloucester from Roman times. From its Roman origins circa AD 40 when the Roman army built a fortress at Kingsholm to the modern city of today, with its magnificent cathedral at its heart, the city remains an historical and cultural hub.

Gloucester was founded as a Roman colonia in AD 96 and at that time the population enjoyed the same status of a Roman citizen. The Romans named the city Glevum and by the second century the city had a planned street layout with impressive and luxurious

DID YOU KNOW THAT...?

The black tiling, which can be seen on the pavement in Westgate Street, represents the layout and position of two former twelfth-century churches. Trinity Church, which stood by the entrance to Bull Lane and St Mary de Grace church, near St John's Lane (formerly Grace Lane). They were both taken down following the Improvement Act of 1750 to make way for the increase in traffic and to make so-called 'improvements'.

Roman buildings. During the Roman occupation, King Lucius, attributed as the first Christian king of Britain, died at Gloucester in AD 181. He is said to be buried in St Mary de Lode church and an effigy in the church is reputed to be of him.

By the fifth century the Romans had left Gloucester and the Anglo-Saxon tribe, the Hwicces, settled in the city founding a monastery in AD 679 dedicated to St Peter. This later became Gloucester Cathedral. By the tenth century Lady Aethelflaed had re-fortified the city and established the street plan, which largely survives today. She was responsible for translating the bones of St Oswald and founding the priory named after him in circa AD 900.

In 1085 William the Conqueror (1028–1087) held a Christmas Court or Christmas Witan in Gloucester, most likely at the Royal Palace of Kingsholm, where he commissioned the Domesday survey. According to the Domesday Book, Gloucester was referred to as a *Civitas et Burgus,* loosely translated to mean an important city.

Gloucester received its first charter from Emperor Nerva who reigned in Gloucester between AD 96 to AD 98. He granted the city the title of Colonia Nervia Glevensis. A colonia was the highest status to be given to a Roman provincial town. Other charters followed. In 1155 Henry II granted the town its first charter of liberties and allowed the burgesses to farm the royal revenues for a period of ten years. In it he stated, 'Wherefore I will and firmly enjoin that my aforesaid burgesses shall have fully all those liberties and free customs and aquittances, so that no one shall do them there in any wrong, shame or damage.' From King John I, the burgesses of Gloucester secured one of the most significant advances in their liberties, a charter of 1200 giving them the right to elect bailiffs and in

The effigy, thought to be that of King Lucius, is dressed in medieval religious garb of alb, stole, maniple and chasuble. It is located in the thirteenth-century chancel of St Mary de Lode church.

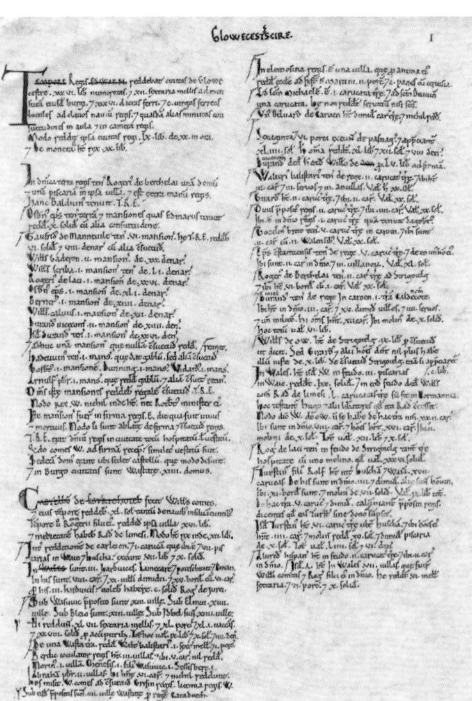
Glowecestscire
I

The city of Gloucester, as it was described in the Domesday Book.

September 1483 Richard III gave the city a major grant of liberties in return for 'the good and faithful actions of the bailiffs and burgesses in causes of particular importance to us.'

In 1580 Elizabeth I granted Gloucester the status of a customs port, boosting the city's maritime trade.

The city of Gloucester enjoys the distinction of two ancient grants of arms. The first, which may be termed the Tudor coat, was granted in 1538. The second, which may be termed the Commonwealth coat, was assigned in 1652.

DID YOU KNOW THAT...?

Following the death of King John, the young Prince Henry was brought to Gloucester. A short account of this historic event is given in Fosbrooke's book.

> When the barons had heard this earle's words [First Earl of Pembroke, William Marshall] after some silence and conference had, they allowed of his saiengs; and immediatlie, wth one consent, proclaimed the young gentleman King of England, whome the Bishops of Winchester and Bath did crowne and anoint, with all due solemnities, at Glocester, upon the day of the Feast of the Apostles Simon and Jude, in presence of the Legat [Cardinal Guala].

Above left: Town of Gloucester. Vert, on a pale or a sword azure, bezanted, the hilt and pommel gules, upon the point a cap of maintenance purpure lined ermine, all between two horseshoes argent pierced sable, each between three nails in triangle argent; on a chief per pale or and purpure a boar's head couped argent, in his mouth a queen apple gules, between two demi-roses, the dexter gules, the sinister argent, both rayed or. [Granted 1538; surrendered 1647]

Above right: Arms: Or three Chevronels between ten Torteaux Gules three three three and one. Crest: Issuant from a Mural Crown Or a demi-Lion guardant Gules holding in his dexter paw a Broadsword and in his sinister paw a Trowel proper. Supporters: On either side a Lion Gules holding in the dexter fore-paw a Broadsword proper. Motto '*Fides Invicta Triumphat*' - Unconquered faith triumphs or Faith indomitable wins through. Arms recorded in 1623, crest and supporters granted in 1652.

Henry III's coronation took place in St Peter's Abbey (Gloucester Cathedral). He became the first and only monarch to be crowned outside of Westminster.

By the Middle Ages, Gloucester was a well-established and thriving city. One description of Gloucester, which adequately describes this fine old city, appears below.

> This city, we found governed by a mayor, with his Sword and Cap of Maintenance, four Maces, twelve Aldermen and a worthy and learned recorder and four stewards. It is walled about, except only that part of the town that is securely and defensively guarded by the river. In the wall there are six gates, for the ingress and egress of strangers and inhabitants. In the midst of the city is a faire cross, whereto from the four Cardinal Winds, the four great and principal streets thereof do come. In her is twelve churches, whereof the cathedral is one.

In this short book I have tried to bring together aspects of Gloucester's great history. Sadly, it was not possible to include everything, for that would require several volumes! My aim, in writing the book, has been to pique the interest of a new generation of Gloucestrians, and visitors, to enjoy this city and to look beyond the modern to the joyous secrets of the past.

Floreat Gloucestrensis!

Let Gloucester flourish!

1. Historic Gloucester

The city of Gloucester has a proud heritage with some of the finest surviving historic buildings to be found in any English city. It boasts the oldest surviving purpose-built library, one of two remaining open-galleried inns and, of course, one of the finest cathedrals in the land.

Roman Times

Glevum, meaning a 'bright place' or 'bright town', was the Roman name for Gloucester and was established from about AD 47. It had long been a prehistoric route of travel but soon became the strategic centre of the west following the Roman occupation. It's hard to believe that the Romans brought elephants to Gloucester – the Roman equivalent of a modern tank – to help them conquer the area. It was here that they built great roads; where the legionaries settled and where men to whom the poetry of Virgil and Horace was familiar and where the flux of commerce in the region began.

The Colonia Nerviana Glevensum

By the end of the first century Emperor Nerva had designated Gloucester as a colonia, the most important type of Roman colonial settlement, reserved specifically for retired soldiers. Archeological excavations have uncovered extensive Roman remains giving a picture of Glevum as a substantial settlement, having grand buildings, which were sumptuously decorated. By the second century Glevum had built public baths in the Westgate Street area with a huge exercise hall, supported by columns of over thirty feet high. A forum and basilica were built and it has also been conjectured that there may have been an amphitheatre, possibly at Gaudy Green outside the Roman walls.

Wall

There are remnants of the original Roman wall scattered around the city centre but none are more accessible than the section to be found in a furniture shop in Southgate Street. The old wooden plaque states it is 'the oldest Roman masonry in Britain.'

Post

The remains of a wooden post, made from solid oak and from the gate tower of the roman legionary fortress built in AD 68 can be seen in the Eastgate Viewing Chamber in Eastgate Street.

This bronze, equestrian statue stands in Southgate Street and was erected in 2002. It was sculpted by the world-renowned Anthony Stones and cast at Pangolin's foundry in Chalford. A stainless steel time capsule is incorporated within the statue's hollow plinth, filled with items relating to the foundation of Roman Gloucester and to life in the present day city.

Part of the original Roman wall dating from the time of Emperor Nerva, which can be found in the Gloucester Furniture Exhibition Centre situated on the corner of Southgate Street and Parliament Street. Just make your way to the left of the store.

Column

Walk past the bank building on the corner of The Cross and Westgate Street and you will see the remains of a Roman column, placed casually in the window of the bank.

Well

Café Rene is a medieval building thought to have been a part of the nearby Greyfriars monastery. In the middle of the bar you will find a Roman well which may have been used by the Franciscan Friars of Greyfriars in 1231. It can be accessed by St Mary's Lane which is alongside St Mary de Crypt churchyard.

Above: You could easily walk past this Roman column without noticing it. Situated in the window of HSBC Bank on The Cross. It is the base of the Roman column in the reception area of the City Museum.

Right: The remarkably preserved remains of a wooden Roman post, which can be seen in the Eastgate Viewing Chamber.

Antonine Plague

In 2004, the remains of ninety-one men, women and children were found on the site of the Church of St Mary Magdalene in London Road. They are thought to have been victims of the Antonine plague which swept through the country in the second century. The find is the first officially recognised Roman mass grave in Britain. Two first-century sculptured and inscribed tombstones were found at the site. One was for a fourteen-year-old slave and the other was for Lucius Octavius Martialis, a soldier of the Twentieth Legion, which was stationed at Gloucester until AD 70.

King's Bastion

The King's Bastion lies beneath the pavement in King's Walk shopping centre and is the site of a Roman fortress from the first century, which later became a medieval bastion used for defending the city.

Via Sacra

The Via Sacra, Latin for Sacred Road or Way, was the main and widest street of the forum in ancient Rome and here in Gloucester they have created their very own via sacra. This is a circular walk around the city taking in many of its historic sites. The route attempts to follow the lines of the original Roman City walls and can be recognised by a pattern of wide, dark paving slabs.

The City Walls and Gates

From Roman times the city of Gloucester was well defended, enclosed by thick stone walls and entered only by gates which would have been manned by porters to collect tolls. Visitors to the city would have entered through no less than six gates. The road from Painswick and the Barton Street suburb were entered by the East Gate, or Ailes Gate. Travellers from Bristol would have entered by the South Gate and if coming from Wales or Hereford the traveller would have crossed the Foreign Bridge, then across a second bridge called Westgate Bridge and on through the West Gate into the city. If you were travelling from London you would have entered via the North Gate with a further outer gate called the Lower North Gate which stood in the London Road. There were three smaller gates in the city, Blind Gate, entered via Water Street in the west of the city and Alvin Gate which stood at the north end of Hare Lane and Postern Gate, where there was a kennel for keeping the hounds that belonged to the city. A further gate called St Oswald's stood near the priory of the same name.

It is a great shame that the city walls were almost entirely demolished following the Siege of Gloucester by Charles II as a punishment because the city supported the parliamentarians.

The Gate Streets

Referred to today as The Gate Streets, North, South, East and West Gate streets still closely follow the line laid down by the Romans, almost 2,000 years ago. At the intersection of these

Part of the *via sacra* showing the distinctive black slabs which mark the way. The brass plaque marks the entrance to the King's Bastion.

streets, stood The High Cross. As you walk the gate streets you will become acquainted with many of the city's historic buildings and trades but also some of its historic oddities.

The High Cross

During the Middle Ages, the city of Gloucester was peppered with preaching crosses, of all types, the most impressive being The High Cross or the *alta crux*.

At 34.5 feet tall, it stood on the intersection of North, South, West and East Gate streets. Although The Cross was taken down in the eighteenth century the intersection where it once stood is still referred to as The Cross in Gloucester. It was called The High Cross to distinguish it from other preaching crosses that were scattered throughout the city in medieval times. Originally, it would have been a fairly simple cross with an octagonal plinth and two storeys, surmounted by a spire with the upper storey having crocketed niches as illustrated by Robert Cole, the cannon of Llanthony Priory in the 1455 Rental of Gloucester.

By 1750, it had become a substantial structure, with a lower storey of blind crocketed arches, an upper storey of eight crocketed niches containing statues of sovereigns, and an elaborate top stage with castellations and pennants. The statues on the cross were listed as those of King John, Henry III and Eleanor his queen, Edward III, Richard II, Richard III, Elizabeth I and Charles I. The choice of John, Henry III, Richard II, and Richard III was probably in recognition of the charters of liberties granted by those kings, and of Queen Eleanor for her tenure of the lordship of the borough during her widowhood. An

The alta crux as it looked in 1455, illustrated by Robert Cole, Canon of Llanthony Priory in the 1455 Rental of Gloucester.

Act of Parliament in 1749 gave permission to demolish several buildings and enlarge the market place and the city's streets. It was deemed necessary to remove The High Cross in order to make these so called improvements. The fate of the cross remains a mystery to this day. Despite extensive research over the centuries no-one can say what happened to it. It was probably broken up and re-used elsewhere.

Westgate Street

This street, once called Ebridge Street, led eventually to the West Gate and the two bridges, which spanned the River Severn, in medieval times. It was the main access for visitors from Wales and Herefordshire.

Pinch Belly Alley

This narrow alley runs between Westgate Street and Cross Keys Lane. It's easy to miss but is one of the oldest alleys in Gloucester. Dating from the tenth century it still has one of the medieval stones, which can be seen in the lane, jutting out slightly. These were placed there, apparently, to prevent errant animals, on market days, from 'doing a runner' and this is how the alley got its name. Since then, the alley has had a number of names including Love Alley (I wonder why?) Foxes Entry or Alley and Mercers' Entry or Alley.

Mercer's Hall

Walk down Pinch Belly Alley and you will come to this building on the right. Although it doesn't look much from the outside this is a very old building, with timbers in the roof having been dated to the late fifteenth century. It has had a variety of occupants, including a perfumier, a cider merchant, a brewer and was once owned by Washbourn Brothers and used as a bonded store for wines and spirits. It is now used as a Masonic Hall.

Maverdine Lane

Hidden behind a Georgian façade and extending for some distance along a narrow alley lies one of the most substantial timber-framed merchants' houses to have survived in any English town. This building is notable for the quality of its surviving detail which includes rare and original patterned leaded glass which you can see if you look upwards from within the alley. Once owned by Alderman John Browne, the first-floor front room was wood-panelled, with the Browne coat of arms displayed on the overmantel. In 1772 it was owned by William Bishop, a grocer and from 1886 to 2015 it was owned by Winfields, the Seed Merchants until it was sold recently to a private buyer.

The Fleece Undercroft

This twelfth-century barrel-vaulted undercroft, beneath the Fleece Hotel, has been part of Gloucester's culture for 600 years. It is an exceptionally fine and early surviving example of its type and is part of the surviving merchant's house above which originally extended westward to Bull Lane, and was recorded in the Rental of 1455 as a great tenement that had belonged to Benedict the Cordwainer in the reign of Henry III. The property above

Believe it or not, this building, in its entirety, stands in Westgate Street hidden behind a Georgian façade. This sketch, drawn by F. W. Waller in 1877, shows the extent of this substantial timber-framed merchant's house

is believed to have been developed as an inn circa 1500 by St Peter's Abbey, and is first recorded as the Golden Fleece Inn in 1673.

Beatrix Potter Museum

The building which houses the museum is early sixteenth century and will be forever linked to the public house, the Tailor of Gloucester, which still stands on the opposite side of Westgate Street. The pub, no longer called the Tailor of Gloucester, was once occupied by J. S. Pritchard who was a tailor and the inspiration for Beatrix Potter's book of the same name.

St Michael's Gate

This fourteenth-century gateway was one of the entrances into St Peter's Abbey and led directly to the Pilgrim's Door where visiting pilgrims would queue to pray at the tomb of Edward II. The gate adjoins the Beatrix Potter Museum.

Gloucester Mint

There has been a mint in Gloucester since the reign of Alfred the Great (871–899) until the end of the reign of Henry III in 1272, marking out Gloucester as an important city. We know from Domesday that King William drew £20 from the mint as the annual rent.

Top: An old postcard showing the vaulted undercroft under the Fleece Hotel in Westgate Street when it was being used as a bar, known locally as The Monk's Bar.

Above: Mosaic tile, by artist Gary Drostle, depicting the trade of a tailor and draper. Intimately linked with the Gloucester inspired story of *The Tailor of Gloucester* by Beatrix Potter. This tile can be found in Southgate Street.

Left: A view of St Michael's Gate with the Beatrix Potter Museum in the background.

The mint was said to have stood close by Holy Trinity church in Westgate Street, near Bull Lane. The earliest known coin of Gloucester is a penny of Alfred the Great (872–901) which can now be found in the British Museum. The custom of providing the name of the actual moneyer on the reverse of the coin gives us more information about the mint and the men who worked there. The names of four moneyers are listed in a manuscript preserved by the British Museum. They were:

1245: Roger l'Enveyse
1249: Richard le Francois
1252: John fitz Simon
1254: Lucas Cornubiensis

A recent find in nearby Highnam of a small silver penny struck at Gloucester in 1080 from the time of William the Conqueror (1066–1087) features the name of the moneyer Silacwine and adds to our knowledge of the operation of the mint.

The Boothall

This ancient guildhall stood on the site of the present Shire Hall on the south side of Westgate Street, in the block between Berkeley Street and Upper Quay Lane. Inside it was a lofty, barn-like structure, supported by double rows of chestnut timber pillars and a set of official weighing beams. Outside, it was constructed of lath and plaster and had many windows as you can see from the drawing below.

Thomas Dudley Fosbrooke, in his book, *An Original History of the City of Gloucester*, describes a scene within the Boothall, which at the time he found remarkable:

> In this ancient hall was transacted a scene perhaps unique in judicial history, viz. a female sitting as a judge. During the quarrels between Anne Lady Berkeley and her relatives, she fled, to her old master, King Henry VIII. Who granted her a special commission under the great seal, to enquire, heare, and determine these riots and other misdemeanors, and made her one of the commissioners and of the quorum; whereupon she came to Gloucester, and there sate on the bench in the publique sessions-hall, impanelled a jury, received evidence, found Sir Nich. Poynz and Maurice Berkeley and their fellows guilty of divers riots and disorders, and fined them.

Over time, the building had a number of uses including, use as an exchange; sittings of the hundred court; as a market hall; a leather market in 1273, and by 1396 wool was sold there and weighed on the official weighing beams. In 1455, the building included an inn, aptly named, the Boothall Inn. Later uses included being used by for concerts, plays, and performances by travelling showmen; a music hall, skating rink, theatre, and cinema and as a coach house and stables for the Boothall Hotel. Finally, in 1957, the hall and the Boothall Hotel were demolished.

Above: The most recent discovery of a coin minted in Gloucester and containing the moneyer's name, Silacwine

Left: This drawing first appeared in the *Illustrated London News* in 1847. This sprawling, medieval building once stood on the site of the Shire Hall.

Dick Whittington Tavern

Hidden behind a Georgian façade is this very important late medieval merchant's house. Now a public house it was previously in the ownership of the Whittington family of Pauntley whose famous son, Richard Whittington, became Mayor of London. Dick Whittington was born around 1350 in Gloucester to William Whittington, Lord of Pauntley. When he was thirteen he was sent to London to be apprenticed to John Fitzwarren. Later he was to become the greatest merchant in medieval England. He supplied silks from Peking for the wedding dresses of the daughters of Henry IV and also lent money to the king. He did become mayor of London four times, in 1397, 1398, 1407 and 1420.

On the first floor of the pub, off the stair landing, a recess to the right has been opened and framed to expose part of a decayed fifteenth-century, possibly sixteenth-century, wall painting, probably a townscape, on plaster. There's also, off the corridor on the east side of the wing, a room with a mid-seventeenth-century panelled dado of which several sections have been removed to expose a late-sixteenth-century painted dado of fruit, flowers and foliage on plaster, possibly the lower portion of a full height scheme of painted decoration. The sixteenth-century fresco decoration is a rare and significant survival.

Folk Museum

This building is one of my all-time favourites in Gloucester. It was built as a merchant's house around 1500, probably for a master clothier and is now the home of the Folk Museum. The building is worth a visit just to see the interior. On every floor much of the

The preserved fresco on an interior wall in the Dick Whittington Public House, which once belonged to the Whittington family of Pauntley.

timber-framing is exposed including the chamfered bridging beams and joists, with some of the timbers retaining their original dark red paint finish. In the rear wing, on the ground floor is wall plaster painted with fleur-de-lys and Tudor roses. On the first floor, the larger chamber has remains of a wall painting of white grotesques on a black background, and a fireplace with a stone-stop chamfered surround.

The house is traditionally believed to have been the lodging for Bishop Hooper the night before he was executed by being burned at the stake. To commemorate this event there is a central rectangular stucco panel with a moulded frame inscribed 'Bishop Hooper's Lodging'.

Westgate Bridge

The original medieval bridge was probably built in the reign of Henry II and was constructed with five great arches. The bridge, crossed the central branch of the Severn at the western limit of the town. A free-standing gatehouse on the east end of Westgate Bridge was one of several connected bridges and causeways across the wide floodplain of the River Severn.

Eastgate Street

Eastgate Street has been known by various names over the years. Iuwenestret, Ailesgate and at one time Jewry Street, as it was once the area where Goucester's medieval Jewish Community lived.

Left: The Folk Museum in Upper Westgate Street where Bishop Hooper is reported to have stayed the night before his execution.

Below: An engraving by C. Catton dated 1798. Two trows navigating Westgate Bridge. The boat on the right has taken down its mast – a distinctive feature of the Gloucester Trow. St Nicholas's church and St Peter's Abbey can be seen in the background.

Bottom: Eastgate Street as it once looked. St Michael's church is in the bottom left corner of the picture. The synagogue was thought to be nearby in a substantial stone house.

The Jewish Quarter

Like most major cities in England, Gloucester had its own medieval Jewry. They lived mainly in Eastgate Street, close to The Cross, which at that time was called Jewry Street. Once a thriving and prosperous community, the Jews were expelled from Gloucester in 1275 by Queen Eleanor because she did not want any Jews living in her dower towns.

Several properties in Eastgate Street are known to have been owned by members of the Jewish community and one character called Mirabelle owned a property opposite Gloucester Mint in Westgate Street. There is a remarkable picture of Mirabelle, drawn in the margin of the 1217/1218 Fine Roll, which can be seen online. The Fine Rolls recorded offers of money to the king for concessions and favours. It's possible it may have been drawn by the then Sheriff, Ralph Musard.

An ancient building, built with pointed arches and used as a cellar, stood close to St Michael's church on the north side of Eastgate Street, and was possibly used as a synagogue.

Gloucester Market Portico

Markets in Gloucester are of ancient origin. It has been said that the right to hold a market in Gloucester existed before the Norman Conquest in 1066. The city holds a charter dating from AD 1155 and a further charter of King Edward I, in 1302, granting the city rights to hold a market in the town. Originally, markets would have been held in The Gate Streets but now the main market in Gloucester is an indoor market. The entrance to this market is an original Corinthian style portico designed by local architects Welland and Maberly and built in 1856 by William Jones & Son. It was removed from its original site to its present site in Eastgate Street and rebuilt. Look up and you will see a magnificently tall, three-bayed arcade designed in the Monumental Italianate style. In the centre is a clock, supported by seated figures sculpted in high relief. Father Time is on the right and *Ceres*, goddess of agriculture, grain crops, fertility and motherly relationships, on the left. At the feet of both figures are realistically carved market produce. The original wrought iron gates are to be found outside the Amey Depot in Eastern Avenue, Gloucester.

DID YOU KNOW THAT...?

There was a Blood Libel accusation, an act of medieval anti-semitism, in 1167, when the body of young boy called Harold was found dead by the River Severn with signs of ritual crucifixion. A fourteenth-century manuscript written by Abbot Frocester, some 200 years later, and held in the library at Gloucester Cathedral details the incident. He is buried in Gloucester Cathedral and was made a martyred saint by the Catholic Church. His saint day is 25 March.

Above: The impressive Corinthian portico, made from Bath stone, built as the entrance to the old Eastgate Market in 1856, rebuilt here in 1973. The inscription reads, 'The Earth is the Lords and the Fulness Thereof'.

Left: Due to its proximity to the river, fish markets were held here in the thirteenth century. This mosaic by artist Gary Drostle, depicts a fishmonger plying their trade in Southgate Street.

DID YOU KNOW THAT…?

In 1760, the sale of a wife took place in Gloucester. It seems that some people believed that if a wife were taken to market on market day often with a halter or sometimes a rope around her neck the transfer was legal. Gloucester magistrates heard the case of a woman who had married in the 1740s. She and her husband did not take long to part by means of a wife sale in Gloucester. Her new husband was a coal miner, Nicholas Read, who took her to Bath, where they were married 'by one parson Crey, a lawless minister there'.

Blue Coat School

This school, opened in 1668, in a house on the north side of Eastgate Street where the Guildhall now stands. The school was founded by Sir Thomas Rich, a native of Gloucester who became a wealthy London merchant engaged in trade with Turkey. In his will, dated 1666, he gave the house to the City Corporation to be used as a school. The endowment, in part, was to provide annual payments of £160 for lodging and maintaining twenty poor boys, £20 for the salary of a schoolmaster to teach the boys reading and writing, and £60 for apprenticing and clothing six of the boys each year. The boys, who were to be dressed in the blue uniform of Christ's Hospital, London, were to stay in the school between the ages of ten and sixteen. The corporation decided to admit only sons of freemen.

The Guildhall

Gloucester's historic Guildhall was originally built in 1890 by George H. Hunt in the French Renaissance style for Gloucester City Council on the site formerly occupied by Sir Thomas Rich's Blue Coat School. On the ground floor it housed offices for the town clerk, accountant, surveyor and other officials. With council chambers, committee rooms, the mayor's parlour and a public hall on the first floor. The Mayor's Ball, which was a grand affair, was held each year in what is now the theatre and remained in use for council meetings and as the Chief Executive's offices until 1985. It is now Gloucester's premier music venue.

Oil on canvas painting by local artist, John Kemp, showing the Blue Coat School in Eastgate Street. John Kemp (1833–1923) was a local Gloucester artist. He was the Principal of Gloucester College of Art during the late nineteenth century.

DID YOU KNOW THAT...?

At the end of Barton Street was the World's End. This was the name given to the last inns in a neighbourhood, which were often brothels. The sign to such hostelries was commonly a man and woman walking together, with the accompanying verse 'I'll go with my friend to the World's End'. In 1658, a building called World's End was recorded in Barton Street which was later divided into three dwellings, one of which, in 1780, became the Red Lion Inn. By the late eighteenth century, World's End became a general term for the area.

Southgate Street

In medieval times, Southgate Street was the site of the city's pillory and stocks. It led to the South Gate, the main entrance into the city for visitors coming from Bristol or the West Country.

The Tolsey

> The ancient Tolsey consisted of a wooden piazza below, with antic figures over the capitals, an overhanging story, with immense sashes, and a balustrade above. It receded in two sides of a triangle from the High Cross.

The Tolsey building stood on The Cross, described here by Fosbrooke. Although a tolsey can be either a tollbooth, a merchants' meeting place or an exchange, it would seem Gloucester's Tolsey, which stood on The Cross, had a number of uses. According to Bishop Kennett it was the place where the lord of the manor received his dues, rents and profits of the fair or market. It was also where 'the Sheriffs may hold all and singular the same pleas from, hour to hour and day to day in the Tolsey court of the city'. It was a meeting place where the mayor and aldermen met and transacted public business and in 1507, there is a suggestion that it was the place where property deeds were filed.

It also the place where on the tenth of August 1643, during the Civil War, the king's Heralds At Arms read out this message to the citizens of Gloucester.

> Out of our tender compassion to our city of Gloucester, and that it may not receive prejudice by our army, which we cannot prevent, if we be compelled to assault it; we are personally come before it to require the same, and are graciously pleased to let all the inhabitants of, and all other persons within that city, as well souldiers as others know ; that if they shall immediately submit themselves and deliver this city to us, we are contented freely and absolutely to pardon every one of them, without exception: and doe assure them, on the word of a King...

In 1892, The Tolsey was replaced by the new Guildhall.

The Bell Inn

Built for Thomas Yate, apothecary and alderman of Gloucester in 1664. On the first floor is a notable mid-nineteenth-century moulded fire surround, carved with cherubs and cornucopia with a segmental pediment to the overmantel, highlighted by the arms of Yate crossed with Berkeley and dated 1650.

Of particular note is the outstanding architectural quality of its carved and panelled timber façade. Fine traces of colour in the grain show that this woodwork was once painted an orange russet colour. The date on the overmantel commemorates the date of his first marriage in 1650. It has been suggested that the first four sons are portrayed as cherubs in the plasterwork and that the other heads show Thomas and his two wives. In the nineteenth century the property was known as the Old Blue Shop, when it was the property of a bluemaker named James Lee. Traces of a dark-grey-blue substance have been found on the facade and under the floor board. Bluemakers manufactured a type of blue dye, principally used by calico printers.

This building was also the birthplace of George Whitefield in 1714.

Cross Keys Lane

Tucked away down this ancient lane, formerly known as Scroddelone or Scrudde Lane, is the Cross Keys Inn, a sixteenth-century-building, which has been a public house since at least the eighteenth century. The lane itself was a centre for the cloth industry in the tenth century.

Robert Raikes' House

A superb example of a later sixteenth-century town house belonging to Robert Raikes. The *Gloucester Journal* was first published from this building by Robert Raikes, Senior on 9 April 1722. Raikes moved his printing office here in 1758, transferring it from Blackfriars.

The Pillory

This largely wooden structure of medieval punishment stood in Southgate Street near St Mary de Crypt church. Miscreants would be shackled to it and in the old tradition of *schadenfreude* people would throw rotten vegetables at them.

Northgate Street

Northgate Street and Hare Lane were the areas where tanners and cordwainers carried on their trade. The River Twyver ran close by, an essential resource for their trade.

The New Inn

Built in 1450 on the site of an old inn hence its name, it was built as a hostelry by the monks of St Peter's Abbey to accommodate the many pilgrims coming to the city to visit the tomb of Edward II.

Pilgrims were accommodated in large rooms on the first and second floors, which could sleep between forty and sixty people to a room. It is the most complete surviving example of a medieval courtyard inn with open galleries in Britain. On the first floor, there is an example of a fine Tudor ceiling, being a later addition to the building. At the

Above: This is an old postcard of the Oak Room in the Bell Inn, showing the elaborately carved fireplace, which can still be seen today in what is now known locally as the Vodka Bar on the first floor.

Left: This meticulously restored building, was once the home of Robert Raikes, the founder of the Sunday School Movement.

Above: Mosaic tile, by artist Gary Drostle, of the skilful trade of a cordwainer. A Cordwainer is a highly skilled craftsman who uses the finest goatskin leather from Cordoba in Spain.

Right: A drawing of the pillory, by Robert Cole, Canon of Llanthony Secunda Priory, which stood in Southgate Street.

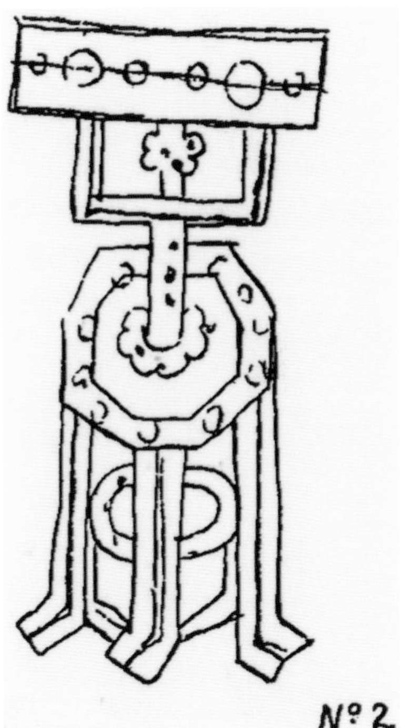

time of dissolution the inn passed to the Dean and Chapter of Gloucester Cathedral and was leased to various innkeepers until it was sold in 1858.

The Tanners' House

This medieval building was discovered in the seventies when the relief road was being built. It is easy to miss as, in its present state, it is almost completely derelict, most of it having been demolished to make way for Stretton's Garage. It is probably the oldest surviving, non-religious building in the city. Dated from the thirteenth century it was built close by the River Twyver, to utilise a constant supply of water, essential for the tanning industry. Four tanning vats were discovered in front of the building.

Court of Probate

This quirky little building sits on the corner of Pitt Street and was cleverly designed by Fulljames & Waller in 1858 and described as 'one and two storeys designed for romantic medieval effect'. It was originally the Court of Probate and was probably built in response to the Probate Act of 1857. There is an inscription in a stone panel in raised Gothic lettering, which reads 'Gloucester Court of Probate MDCCCVIII'.

The Building News of 1861 reported that it was:

> Erected by Thomas Holt, Esq., the diocesan registrar and secretary to the Bishop of Gloucester and Bristol, from designs furnished by Fulljames and Waller, of Gloucester. Mr. Oliver Estcourt was the builder, and the cost was £1,100. In addition to the offices

This fine example of an open-galleried inn, stands proudly on the corner of Northgate Street and New Inn Lane, formerly called Pilgrim's Lane, and still looks remarkably as it does in this drawing.

A sketch by John Clarke of the Tanners' House as it looked in 1850.

connected with the Court of Probate there are other private rooms. There is a large strong-room covered with a fireproof roof, situate at the back of the premises, but connected with the main building.

City Museum and Art Gallery

This building was originally the Price Memorial Hall, built as a lecture hall for the Gloucester Science and Art Society in 1893 by F. S Waller for Margaret Hall as a memorial to her husband William Edwin Price who was MP for Tewkesbury and who died at the age of forty-four. It was designed in an eclectic early Renaissance style inspired by the work of T. G. Jackson. The most important internal feature of the original building is the main ceiling at eaves level, coved with three sun-burner centrepieces. The interior also includes part of the scheduled Roman colonia wall. In 1902 it was adapted for use as a museum and art gallery for the Corporation of the City of Gloucester.

Court of Probate as it is today, much unchanged, showing the hard-to-read Gothic lettering of the inscription.

Public Library

Built in the Gothic style of the thirteenth century, by Fulljames, Waller and Son in 1872, it was funded mainly by subscribers. It was converted and extended between 1897 and 1900 for the Corporation of the City of Gloucester when it became a public library.

The Spa

In 1747, quite by accident, during the sinking of a well in the garden of Eagle Hall in Lower Westgate Street, the spa waters of Gloucester were first discovered. It was not until 1787 that the new occupier, Mr John Lewis realised the medicinal qualities of this water. The waters were analysed by a Dr John Hemming who published a book on the matter. His imminent findings were announced, with much excitement, in the *Gloucester Journal* on 29 June 1789:

> The proprietor of the Glocester Spa begs leave most respectfully to inform the nobility and gentry, and the public in general, that Dr. Hemmings' Analysis upon the medicinal virtues of the water, in which will be mentioned a number of remarkable cures performed by the said water, will be out of the press this week.

Mr Lewis went on to build a pump room but its popularity was to be shortlived. In 1814, a Mr Jelf, who ran Gloucester Old Bank, discovered springs on the south side of the city. He sank wells, built a pump room with hot and cold baths, and laid out walks. Shortly afterwards, Jelf was made bankrupt. However, the spa gained a reprieve from wealthy investors until, in time, they too got into financial difficulties, partly as a result of the cholera epidemic of 1832 and partly the victim of the growing industrial docks. The Spa Hotel, which would later become Ribston Hall, was built by the spa company in 1818 as a boarding house specifically for visitors to the spa. Elizabeth Barratt Browning was a guest in the former Spa Hotel for a year during her convalescence. The spa proprietors sold it in 1835 and from 1860 it was a college for young ladies called Ribston Hall.

Eventually the spa closed and the building was finally demolished in 1960.

Above: The public library with its tall four-light window with transom and trefoiled heads to the lights; the frame of the window is crowned by a blind, cinquefoiled arch enclosing an armorial shield, which is one of the city's coat of arms.

Left: This ornamental pineapple is all that remains of the glorious Gloucester Spa. You can view it in the gardens of Gloucester Folk Museum.

Wotton House

This large house, now a nurses' home, was built for Thomas Horton in 1707. The house and extensive grounds can be seen in an engraving by Kip dated 1712. The house and its owners have an interesting history.

Thomas Horton was the son-in-law of John Blanch who was MP for Gloucester between 1710 and 1713. Thomas died in 1727. At his death, he is recorded as being a 'lunatic'. He was succeeded by his son, also called Thomas, who sadly was also declared a 'lunatic' in 1746. His estates, which were placed in the custody of his brothers-in-law, were disputed after Thomas's death in 1755 for, although by will dated 1735, he had left them to members of the Brereton family, in 1739 he had settled them on his two sisters. Agreement for a threefold partition was reached in 1758, and in 1763 Wotton House was confirmed as part of the share of the Revd. Richard Brereton who enlarged the estate and died in 1801.

The formal gardens, which can be seen in Kip's illustration, were destroyed by the nineteenth century, only the outer walls remain. In 1925 it was acquired by Gloucestershire County Council and converted as a hostel for its School of Domestic Science. Gloucestershire Area Health Authority bought the house in the late 1970s.

Hillfield House

Built by Albert Estcourt, a master local builder, for Charles Walker, who was a local timber merchant in 1867. An earlier house called Woodbine Hill stood on the grounds. The park was opened to the public around 1933 and is home to three monuments of historical significance, Scriven's Conduit, the King's Board and the chancel of the twelfth-century leper chapel of St Mary Magdalene. The remnants of a Roman road have also been unearthed on the site.

The building is particularly noted for its elaborately carved interior and the level of detail which went into the building of this house. Bronze railings, made in France, and the floor laid with Sicilian and black marble. The stairwell is dominated by two semi-circular, arched and moulded stone windows with richly coloured stained glass.

Robinswood Hill Cross

It's strange to think that there were once a series of reservoirs at the foot of Robinswood Hill and that a single spring supplied the city's water for more than 400 years. Perhaps the naming of Reservoir Road gives us the clue as to the siting of these reservoirs. At some point, possibly in the thirteenth century, a stone of 'massive proportions' was placed across the source of the spring to protect it. Cut in the form of a cross with inclined planes it measured 6 foot, 8 inches in length, 1 foot and 4.5 inches in width and the transom measured 2 foot 11 inches. A small wooden door was fixed into the structure to gain access to the spring.

The Royal Palace of Kingsholm

Gloucester once had its own Royal Palace at Kingsholm. It is well known that English kings have stayed there. In 1051 Edward the Confessor summoned his magnates to his 'palace at Gloucester'. It is said that William the Conqueror in 1085 held the Christmas Witan there where he ordered the Domesday Survey. The Saxon palace complex was used for national assemblies and must have been large for when it was first identified in the eighteenth century, following a find of the remains of a ruined building in Kingsholm Close, the building was found to measure 120 foot square. A hoard of more than half a

These stained glass windows were made by Lavers and Barraud and depict subjects from Gloucester's history, principally Sheriff Sir William Tracy and Robert of Gloucester. They bear the initials of the owner, C. W., and the year of construction, 1867. At the bottom of the window is the Heraldic crest of the Walker family and the motto *cura et industria*.

The only horizontal, solid stone cross in Gloucestershire, still in situ on Robinswood Hill.

peck of Saxon coins was found in the same field sometime before 1785, and many other Saxon coins have been found there.

Gloucester Castle

Gloucester is said to have had two castles. The first, built soon after the Conquest was a timber and earthwork castle, built in the south west corner of the Roman walled town, using the surviving Roman wall. The second, a stone castle, was built outside the Roman town wall, on the site where the present prison stands. It was first documented in

Domesday, where it is recorded that sixteen houses were demolished to make room for it. It became a Royal Castle in 1155. Henry III stayed there often and in 1214 Queen Isabella of Angoulême, King John's wife, was imprisoned there until his death in 1216.

During excavations in 1983 a wooden board game was found on the site of the castle, complete with thirty playing counters, using themes such as astrological symbols, biblical scenes and animals. Based on the game of backgammon, it incorporates panels of thin bone, displaying scenes of dragons and serpents and dates from the early medieval age.

The wooden board game found on the site of the old Gloucester Castle dates to the twelfth century.

2. Religious Gloucester

Gloucester has been a religious centre since the first monastery was founded in the city in AD 678 by Osric, an Anglo-Saxon prince. That monastery was St Peter's Abbey, later to become Gloucester Cathedral.

St Peter

Around the year AD 678, Osric, who became King of Northumbria, founded the monastery of St Peter. A noblewoman by the name of Kyneburga, became the first Abbess. A recent statue of Kyneburgha, unveiled in 2013, can be seen in the cathedral. The abbey survived the dissolution of the monasteries and became The Cathedral Church of St Peter and the Holy and Indivisible Trinity, or Gloucester Cathedral as it is popularly known, ensuring the continuity of religious worship on this site.

St Oswald

St Oswald's Priory was founded by Lady Aethelflaed of Mercia, daughter of Alfred the Great, around AD 900. It was originally dedicated to St Peter but in AD 909 the relics

The cathedral's cloister garden, showing the tower built in the Perpendicular style during the fifteenth century.

of Saint Oswald were translated there by Aethelflaed and her husband Athelred. Archaeological excavations in the 1970s revealed a tenth century fragment of carved slab from the grave of someone who had been extremely important. It is widely acknowledged that Aethelflaed and her husband were buried in the crypt. Having survived the Dissolution of the Monasteries the priory was largely destroyed by Royalist cannon fire during the Siege of Gloucester.

Blackfriars

Blackfriars Priory was founded in 1239 by Sir Stephen de Hermshall and largely built with funds and materials donated by King Henry III. The friars of this Dominican order were called Blackfriars because of the distinctive black cappas they wore. The priory contains the oldest surviving, purpose built library, or scriptorium.

After the dissolution, in 1539, the buildings of the friary were sold to Thomas Bell, the wealthy Gloucester capper and clothier.

Found in a wall near St Oswald's Priory, Gloucester, this cross fragment is dated to the tenth century. The left hand shows the original, the right hand shows the false colour version to pick out the figures and knots.

The fine scissor-braced roof in the nave of the priory made from oak donated by the king from the Royal Forest of Dean.

Greyfriars

Very little remains of this medieval monastic house. It was founded in 1231 with the help of Thomas I of Berkeley, who gave them the land and Henry III who donated timbers for building. The Grey Friars, or Franciscans, were followers of St Francis of Assisi. They earned their name from the grey habits that were worn as a symbol of their vow of poverty. Around 1518, Maurice Berkeley, the son of Thomas, who was by then their patron provided funds to rebuild the priory in the perpendicular Gothic style. It did not survive the dissolution and became a brew house. During the Siege of Gloucester the buildings were severely damaged by Royalist forces.

Whitefriars

The house of the Carmelite friars, known as Whitefriars, again because of their distinctive white clothing was founded circa 1268 in all likelihood by Queen Eleanor, together with Thomas de Berkeley and Thomas Gyffard. Built outside of the city walls, near the North Gate and on the site of what is now the bus station, nothing remains of this building. It suffered a similar fate as the other religious orders in the city, being a victim of the dissolution and of the Civil war.

Llanthony Secunda

Llanthony Secunda was founded in 1136 by Miles de Gloucester, the first Earl of Hereford. The family would have a long association with the priory. Miles' daughter, Margaret, married Humphrey de Bohun and they continued the patronage. Several generations of de Bohuns were buried at Llanthony Secunda but in the late 1790s, whilst developing the Gloucester and Berkeley canal, their graves and many of the buildings were destroyed.

Following the dissolution the site was sold by the Crown to Arthur Porter. As with many other historic buildings Llanthony Secunda suffered during the siege of Gloucester in 1643.

St Michael

All that is left of this medieval church, which stood on The Cross is the fifteenth century tower, now home to Gloucester Civic Trust. There had been a church, St Michael the Archangel, on this site since the twelfth century. The tower dates from 1465.

St Mary de Crypt

Only two rounded half pillars give the clue that there has been a church on this site since Norman times when it was first recorded in 1140 as the Church of the Blessed Mary within

The medieval precinct wall of Llanthony Priory still survives. The waymarking cross, in black brick, can be clearly seen.

DID YOU KNOW THAT...?

The surviving precinct wall at Llanthony Secunda Priory is one of the oldest brick structures in Gloucestershire. The evidence for this is barely visible save for a wayside cross of black brick in the brickwork. In addition to serving the function of reiterating and reinforcing the Christian faith amongst those who passed the cross and of reassuring the traveller, wayside crosses often fulfilled a role as waymarkers, especially in difficult and otherwise unmarked terrain. This wayside cross would have shown the way to Gloucester for visitors and pilgrims coming from the south or Bristol.

DID YOU KNOW THAT...?

In 1393 the curfew bell of St Michael's church was rung at 4.00 a.m. and 8.00 p.m. to remind people to put out their fires, as fire was a huge risk because many of the buildings in Gloucester were timber built. In later years the curfew bell may have been used to warn residents of air raids during the Second World War. In 1956, the bells were removed, two were given to the cathedral and the rest were sold.

St Michael's church as it looked *c.* 1819. The church building to the left of the tower has since been demolished.

Southgate. In 1539, benefactors John and Joan Cooke started a school next to the church. The rent for this is still paid annually to the rector of St Mary de Crypt and consists of a single red rose!

The church has played an integral role in the religious life of the city, evidenced by the number of famous people who have been either baptised, educated, preached, taught or buried here. Both George Whitefield and Robert Raikes were baptised here and educated in the church's school. John Biddle, universally known as the Father of English Unitarianism, was the master of Crypt School and Jemmy Wood, the miser, is buried here.

St John the Baptist

It has been said that the ancient church on this site was built by King Athelstan, and consisted of a large nave and south aisle of the same length, a chancel, a large porch on the north side and a slender steeple at the west end of the aisle. In the steeple 'were five bells, and a saint's bell, formerly rung at the elevation of the host, that all persons might then fall on their knees.'

It is stated, in *Rudge's History and Antiquities of Gloucester,* 'that after the battle of Bosworth Field, in 1485, wherein King Richard III was slain, Francis Viscount Lovell and

A copper engraving, by an anonymous artist, published *circa* 1800 of the Grammar School at St Mary de Crypt in Southgate Street.

Lord Stafford fled to this church for sanctuary; but Stowe says, that Francis Viscount Lovell and Humphrey Stafford, with Thomas Stafford, his brother, (not the two Lord Staffords, father and son), took sanctuary in this church.'

All that remains of the medieval church is a small portion of the wall which can be seen in the public toilet at the back of the church.

St Nicholas

This church, first recorded in 1180, stood near the old west gates of the city. It was known as St Nicholas of the Bridge of Gloucester, and belonged to the crown, which suggests that it was founded by a monarch. It was largely rebuilt in the thirteenth century.

Inside is a well preserved and most impressive tomb of John Walton and his wife Alice carved by Samuel Baldwyn, the father of Stephen, who carved the statue of King Charles II. John was a Goldsmith, former City Alderman and Sheriff of Gloucester. He died in 1626, his wife before him in 1620. He wears the red robes of office while his wife Alice has a broad-brimmed hat, worn over a coif, with neck ruffle, of North European influence, stylish at the time. Kneeling by them, at the base of the tomb, are two figures, thought to be their son and daughter. The production of a tomb of this quality for a town alderman and his wife is indicative of the rise of an urban elite and middle class in Gloucester, who turned to portraiture to depict themselves.

On the south door once hung a fourteenth-century closing ring, now in the custody of the City museum.

St Mary de Lode

Lode is an ancient Saxon word, meaning crossing or passage which suggests at the time of its foundation there was a channel of the River Severn nearby, which has now been filled up. Thought to be of Saxon origin because of the name, it is thought to have been built over two substantial Roman buildings. This was confirmed in 1825 when a Roman pavement was discovered and again in 1978 when a large mosaic with a white diagonal trellis decoration against a black background was found. This can be viewed at the rear of the north nave pews.

The exquisite detailing of the clothing of Alice Walton. Her effigy, along with that of her husband's, can be found in the church of St Nicholas, Westgate Street.

It is also the church where the effigy, said to be of King Lucius, is located and where the stake used to burn Bishop Hooper was found in 1826. The charred timber stake can be seen in the Folk Museum.

Chapel of St Mary Magdalene

This tiny chapel in London Road was once the chapel of the former leper hospital of St Mary Magdelene. It was built on the outskirts of the city in the mid-twelfth century to accommodate those returning from the Crusades suffering from leprosy. Inside, set into the floor, is the recumbent effigy of a young lady identified, in error, as that of the Saxon St Kyneburgh as it originated in the long-demolished St Kyneburgh's Chapel at Kimbrose. It is, on stylistic grounds, more likely to represent one of the daughters of Humphrey de Bohun who died young in the thirteenth century, possibly Margaret or Isabella. Outside, by the entrance porch, you can see fine examples of medieval graffiti, thought to be by pilgrims. They include crosses and floral motifs.

Barnwood Cross

Covered almost entirely in sage-coloured lichen and moss and hardly recognisable as a fourteenth-century stone preaching cross, it now stands in plain sight in the grounds of Barnwood Parish church. Originally mentioned in Charles Pooley's book, *Notes on the Old Crosses of Gloucestershire*, published in 1868, this preaching cross was found in a private garden thought to be Barnwood Court.

George Whitefield, 1714–1770

George Whitefield was probably the most famous religious orator on both sides of the Atlantic of the eighteenth century. He was born in the Bell Inn in Southgate Street and christened in the nearby church of St Mary de Crypt. He attended the local Crypt School, a room above St Mary de Crypt church. He was a slight young man of twenty-one with a squint in his eye when he was ordained at Gloucester Cathedral. He went on to study at Pembroke College, Oxford at the age of seventeen but returned to Gloucester due to ill health. Whilst recuperating he drew the attention of the Bishop of Gloucester who later

The remains of the old preaching cross, known as The Barnwood Cross, in its present location at Barnwood Parish church.

ordained him, first as a deacon, then later a priest at Gloucester Cathedral. Whitefield preached his first sermon at St Mary de Crypt Church a week after his ordination. Afterwards, complaints were made to the Bishop of Gloucester that he had driven fifteen people mad with his preaching as his voice was so powerful it could be heard from as far away as a mile. Despite poor health, George had the energy and perseverance of ten men. He drove himself relentlessly, neglecting his health and personal needs in his ambition to tell as many people as he could about Jesus Christ and how faith could change their lives. He was a charismatic speaker who touched the emotions of people in amazing ways. It was said the clarity and sincerity of his message affected everyone he encountered from the nobility to the miners at Bristol.

The most important decision of his career was made when George decided to become a missionary in Georgia in America. He preached in the open air and started at 6.00 a.m., soon gaining a reputation for his oratory. It has been estimated that George Whitefield spoke to a staggering six million people in an age where there were no media aids. He is best known for his efforts at spreading the First Great Awakening in the American Colonies. He became known as 'the apostle of the British Empire'.

Benjamin Franklin, the American statesman, who became a firm friend of George Whitefield wrote about him, 'He is a good man and I love him'.

Finally, exhausted and unwell, George gave his last sermon at the age of fifty-six. He is buried in the Old South Presbyterian Church at Newburyport, Massachusetts in a crypt under the pulpit.

Robert Raikes, 1736–1811

Robert Raikes was born in Ladybellegate House in Gloucester, baptised at St Mary de Crypt church in Southgate Street and educated at Crypt School and then Kings School. When he left he was apprenticed to his father, who at that time was a local printer, who founded the *Gloucester Journal*. When his father died in 1757 he took over as editor of the journal but he is best known for founding the Sunday School Movement. It is said that one day, while looking for a gardener, he found himself in St Catherine's Street, he

The bust of George Whitefield by the distinguished sculptor, John Bacon, in Gloucester City Museum.

noticed a group of ragged children playing there. The gardener's wife told him that it was even worse on Sunday when the street was full of children cursing and swearing and spending their time in noise and riot. He realised that most of these children were employed in the pin making industry in Gloucester, living a deprived life and eventually ending up in Gloucester Prison as a result. Soon after this, he and the Reverend Thomas Stock opened the world's first Sunday school in St Catherine's Street. Any child between the ages of five and fourteen were admitted and lessons were given by suitable ladies who were paid one shilling and sixpence. Their 'lessons' included reading and writing and an obligatory visit to Church. Raikes himself wrote out a schedule for the school's day as reported in Montrose J. Moses 1907 book, *Children's Books and Reading*:

> The children were to come after ten in the morning, and stay till twelve; they were then to go home and return at one; and after reading a lesson, they were to be conducted to Church. After Church, they were to be employed in repeating the catechism till after five, and then dismissed, with an injunction to go home without making a noise.

Raikes reported on the success of his Sunday schools in his newspaper, The *Gloucester Journal* and the model was soon to be adopted throughout the country. Robert Raikes retired in 1802 and died in 1811 of a heart attack. The local children who had attended his Sunday school, also attended his burial in St Mary de Lode church and were each given one shilling and a large piece of Mrs Raike's plum cake. As these schools preceded the first state funding of schools for the general public, they are seen as the forerunners of the current English school system.

In 1844, Nathaniel Hawthorne, American novelist and short story writer wrote *A Good Man's Miracle* about what he called Raikes' efforts as 'a benevolent man's simple and conscientious act on earth, and connects it with those labors of love which the angels make it their joy to pefform, in Heaven above.'

Such was the international impact of Robert Raikes, a statue of him was erected in 1880 on Victoria Embankment in London and one near Queen's Park, Toronto, Ontario, Canada. A replica of the original, created by Sir Thomas Brock RA, was erected in 1930 in Gloucester Park.

Bishop John Hooper, 1495–1555

John Hooper was consecrated as the Bishop of Gloucester on 8 March 1551. He was said to have once been a Friar at Blackfriars Priory in Gloucester in the year 1538. On the death of Edward VI in 1553, Mary Tudor succeeded to the throne and almost immediately Bishop Hooper came to her attention. On the first of September of that same year he was committed into the Fleet prison, followed by six days in Newgate prison. The Bishop of London declared him degraded and 'an obstinate and incorrigible heretic'. Refusing to recant he was sentenced to be burnt at the stake in Gloucester. Arriving in Gloucester he was lodged in the private house of Mr Robert Ingram, said to be the same building which now houses the Gloucester Folk Museum. It was a short walk from here on the morning of 9 February 1555 at about 9.00 a.m. that he was taken to his place of execution, a stake outside St Mary's Gate, by an old Elm tree, beyond the cathedral precinct where he was burnt in front of a crowd of thousands of local people.

The statue, erected in 1930 in Gloucester Park, and dedicated to Robert Raikes, the founder of the Sunday School Movement.

This 1840 painting, by Michael William Sharp R. A., shows the gruesome scene of Bishop Hooper's execution outside St Mary's Gate. The painting is in the Gloucester City Museum's collection.

A memorial monument, dedicated to the memory of Bishop Hooper, was erected in St Mary's Square on the very spot where he was executed. The idea of the monument to Hooper did not arise until 1826, when workmen enlarging St Mary de Lode's churchyard uncovered wood ash and the remains of a large stake on a mound close to St Mary's Gate. Following this incredible discovery a pedestal monument with a plaque dedicated to Hooper was placed on the spot where the stake had been found. By 1851 this monument was in a poor state of repair and a public appeal to raise money to build a new one was launched. Ten years later, sufficient funds had been raised and the Gloucester architects Medland & Maberley were chosen to build it. Their design was for a decorated Gothic style monument with buttressed piers, a tall crocketed spire and a central space for a statue of Hooper. In September 1861, the foundation stone was laid, together with a time capsule containing a dedication letter and coins of the realm, and work was completed the following April, when the vicar of St Mary de Lode Church was called upon to place the stone finial on top of the spire. A competition was then launched to design the statue of Bishop Hooper and in May 1862, models of these were put on public display in the city's

Bishop Hooper's monument, showing him in bishop's garb, underneath the canopy of the monument to him in St Mary's Square.

Assembly Rooms in Westgate Street. The winner was Edward Thornhill from Dublin who carved the statue out of Portland Stone at a total cost of £105. On 14 February 1863, the completed monument was unveiled in a civic ceremony. The monument, a slightly larger than life statue of the Bishop, features decorated angels on the inside of the canopy's arches and numerous grotesque carvings resembling various animals carved into the pinnacles of the buttresses.

The Quakers

The Quakers came to Gloucester in 1655 and held their first meeting at the house of a man called Thomas Rudhall. His son, Abraham, would start the famous Rudhall family bell foundry in Gloucester.

They were not generally welcomed and in 1658 it was recorded that eleven Quakers were being held in the Gloucester County gaol and in 1662, when the Quaker Act was introduced banning meetings of five or more Quakers, this had increased to seventeen.

In 1660, during the interregnum, George Fox, the founder of the Quaker movement came to Gloucester. He described it as 'rude and divided' with some soldiers for the king and some for parliament. Hostility towards the Quakers continued, many of them imprisoned in the city's gaols. They were a small religious community and would have been very visible from their distinctive dress and the way they spoke.

Matters improved for the Quakers in Gloucester and by 1834 they had built the Society of Friends Meeting House, a Georgian building, in Greyfriars. The interior of this building has a rare and unusual room partitioning system, made of mahogany, which is operated by a large brass winding handle.

3. Industrial Gloucester

Gloucester's industrial heritage begins with the Roman occupation, when trade routes were being discovered, it flourished in the medieval age when trade expanded and became an industrial behemoth in the Victorian era.

The medieval trades were that of ironworking, cloth making, and leather. The river allowed for trade routes to open up further afield importing wines from Gascony, spices and cloth from Flanders. Timbers from the Forest of Dean, transported by boat, established the ongoing timber trade along the riverside in Gloucester. One of Gloucester's most important trades was the manufacture of pins, first recorded in the city in 1396. This trade flourished when in 1626 John Tilsby introduced the manufacture of pins into Gloucester and by 1744 it was the main industry employing women and children in the city.

The ironworking trades were reflected in the early city seals displaying horseshoes, nails and swords and the city's streets were often named after local trades, such as Longsmith Street, named after the smith's forges and Bull Lane, near the market or Bell Lane, near the bell foundry.

The principal industry in the 1530s was the capping industry, the knitting of woollen caps, the principal capper being Thomas Bell who purchased Blackfriars after the dissolution and turned it into a cap making factory.

A series of metal pins were commissioned to celebrate the pin-making industry in Gloucester. This is one of the pins, made by artist Matthew Fedden, outside Shire Hall in Westgate Street.

Banking

The Gloucester Old Bank was one of the oldest private banks in England. It operated between 1716 and 1838 and was founded by James Wood. After the death of the first James Wood, the bank passed to his son Richard Wood and on his death in 1802 to his son James Wood, known locally as Jemmy and who would later became known as the famous Gloucester miser. The bank was said to have been the oldest private bank in Britain, having survived the financial consequences of the Napoleonic Wars when many other banks went out of business. At some point in the nineteenth century the bank became the Gloucester City Old Bank. In 1838, it was taken over by the County of Gloucestershire Banking Company which eventually became part of Lloyds Bank.

The bank was a medieval timber building at No. 22 Westgate Street and consisted of a counter within a larger draper's shop.

Other banks followed. In the early 1800s Gloucester had at least five privately owned banks, including Gloucester City Old Bank, which was founded in 1716, the similarly-named Gloucester Old Bank, run by the Nibletts & Jelf partnership, and Gloucester Bank which was owned by John Merrol Stephens. Gloucester Bank had been founded some time before 1793 by two local businessmen named Turner and Morris. In 1837 local merchant William Price, was the founder and director of the Gloucestershire Banking Company.

Timber

Price & Co.

Timber merchants Price & Co. were a family firm established in 1736 by Morgan Price. He passed the business on to his son, William Philip Price who was also a Liberal politician

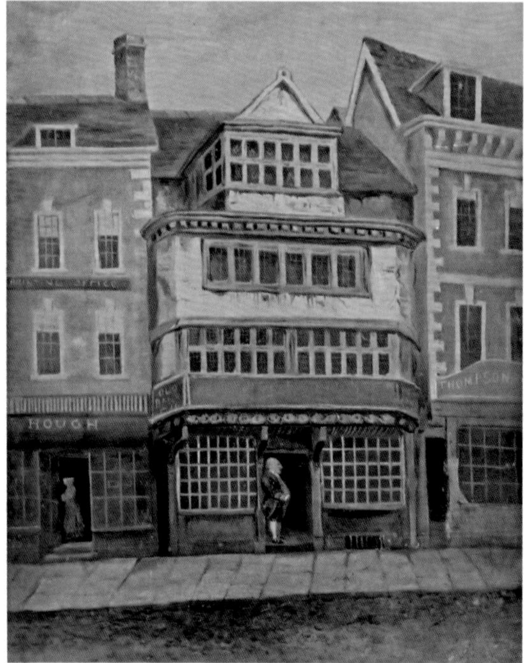

A painting, by J. R. Orton, of the old bank premises at No. 22 Westgate Street. The figure in the doorway is intended to be that of Jemmy Wood.

and MP. Morgan's grandson, William Edwin Price, also a Liberal MP then took over the firm. The company became one of the largest importers of timber in the country, largely due to the opening up of the Sharpness to Gloucester canal in 1827 but also, in part, to the appointment of Charles Walker in 1840 who possessed the necessary business acumen. Walker introduced his son, Charles Betteridge Walker into the firm and his son George Norton Walker succeeded his father.

The company imported timber from Russia, Sweden, Norway, and Canada. During the Crimean War, they supplied the wood for the wooden huts and barracks, used by the French Army.

Messrs Nicks & Co.

William Nicks came to Gloucester in the early 1840s as a traveller for timber merchants Price & Co. There he met Robert Heane, and following a misunderstanding with their managing partner, the two young men broke away to set up their own business in 1849. Trading under the name of Heane & Nicks, they quickly built up a successful business importing timber for the railways being built in the Midlands. William Nicks died in 1855 and having no sons, he passed the business to his son-in-law Albert Buchanan.

Nicks & Co still trade today from the Canada Wharf site in Bristol Road.

Wines and Spirits

Messers Washbourn Brothers

In 1898 the Masonic Hall, formerly known as The Mercer's Hall, was purchased by Messers Washbourn Brothers who used it as a bonded store for wines and spirits. The company had been in existence since at least 1767 when it was mentioned in a document of that date.

The cellars, in Crypt Alley near Bell Lane, which they used for storage consisted of a vaulted passage, 240 feet in length, illuminated by a row of gas jets. Scores of casks and thousands of bottles lined the walls, containing wines and spirits to suit the most fastidious connossieur. Brandy, gin, whiskey from Scotland and champagne were also stored here. In the 1800s, they exported to America, India, South Africa and Malta.

Bells

Bell founding has been a Gloucester industry for over 700 years. The earliest reference is to a burgess called 'Hugh the Bellfounder' in about 1270.

An important late-fifteenth-century bell founder was Robert Hendley, whose name appears on the fourth bell of St Nicholas church, Westgate Street. One of his successors, William Henshawe, was sufficiently important to be five times elected mayor of Gloucester between 1503 and 1520. There is a brass memorial to his two wives in St Mary de Crypt church.

One of the leading foundries in the country during the seventeenth and eighteenth centuries was run by the Gloucester family of Rudhall who, between 1684 and 1835 produced over 5,000 bells in the city. The Rudhalls transported their bells via the local canal system as they could be cheaply and easily transported by barge or ship. Some of the larger bells could weigh anything up to two tons.

Left: The vaulted cellar, described as Bell Lane Cellars, paved with old Roman tiling, being used as a storeroom by wine merchants, Washbourn Brothers.

Below: The mosaic in Southgate Street, outside the entrance to the Eastgate Indoor Shopping centre, citing the bellmaker, William Henshawe, and depicting the making of a bell.

The foundry was started by Abraham Rudhall, a carpenter of Quaker parentage. His bells were often inscribed with phrases such as 'Prosperity to this Parish' together with the date, a decorative border and the founder's initials. His trademark was to place a small bell by his initials. Abraham Rudhall's son was also called Abraham. He obtained the freedom of the city in 1704, which enabled him to work as a fully qualified bell founder. Abel Rudhall, the grandson, carried on the foundry until his death in 1760. Abel Rudhall was succeeded by his younger sons Thomas and Charles. Records place the Rudhall foundry in the area of New Inn Lane, off Northgate Street.

A druggist's mortar, inscribed John Lovett Druggist Gloucester J. R. FEC'T, made by John Rudhall is in the care of Gloucester Folk Museum.

The last bell to be cast at the Gloucester foundry was a miniature bell inscribed with the words Edward Churchill 1833 and John Simpson 1848. This is also housed in the

Gloucester Folk Museum. There is also a bell inscribed I. RUDHALL from the farmhouse at The Downs in Chalford, thought to be cast by Isaac Rudhall, known to have been christened in 1716 in St John the Baptist church, Northgate Street.

Within the cloisters of Gloucester Cathedral are a number of inscriptions relating to the Rudhall family. One describes Abraham as 'a bellfounder famed for his great skill, beloved and esteemed for his singular good nature and integrity'.

Toys

Roberts Brothers

Roberts Brothers of Gloucester was, at one period, considered to be the largest maker of pastimes and games in the United Kingdom. The firm, founded by the brothers Harry Owen Roberts and John Owen Roberts, developed from a simple party game devised by the brothers for a Sunday school class. The game received a patent in 1890, and a publisher was found to market it, soon causing a craze for the game of *Piladex*. Across the Atlantic Piladex was to be franchised as *Pillow Dex*.

In 1894 the brothers decided to concentrate on the growing business as they added more and more games to their repertoire. Following royal patronage, the firm expanded leading to the brothers building a state-of-the art factory in the city in 1902. They adopted the trade name of Glevum, based on the Roman name for Gloucester, and soon began to use a stylised

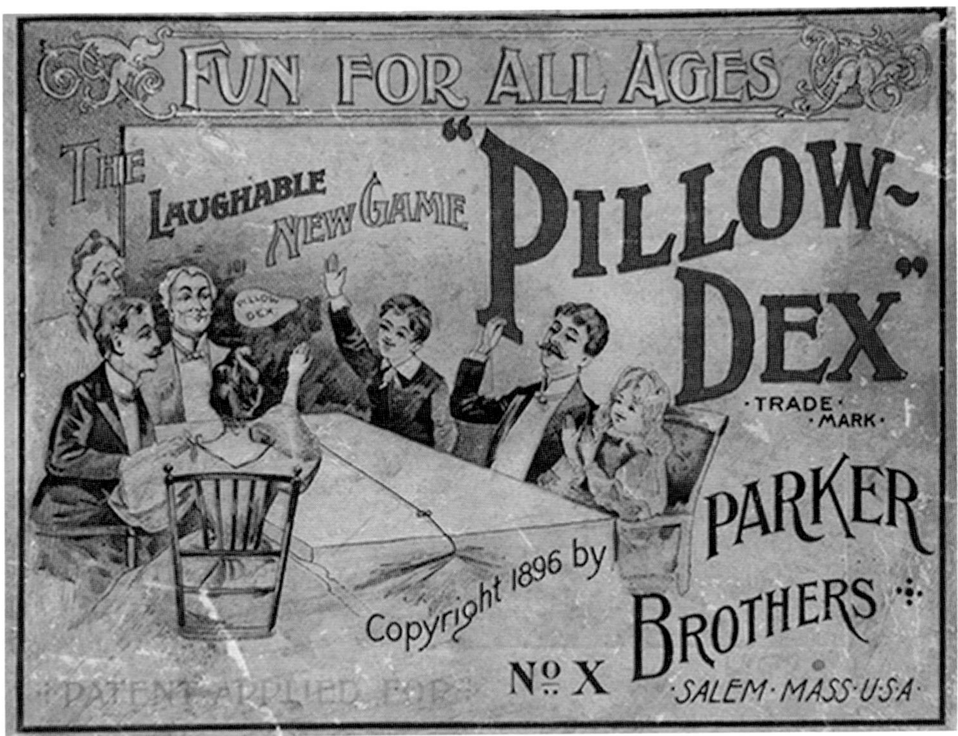

The American version of Piladex, franchised in 1896 as Pillow Dex and produced in the US by Parker Brothers.

head of a Roman soldier as the trade mark. The company continued to grow, despite the First World War and the Depression. Agencies and offices were found across the world, and at the height of its success more than 750 were employed. The Second World War was to provide a halt to their growth. The factory was commandeered for war work, and all but a handful of staff went into the forces or other areas supporting the war effort. After the war the company's fortunes were slow to recover, and as a result of a number of factors the directors were forced to seek a friendly take-over by rivals Chad Valley, resulting in the effective end of the company in 1956 with the factory finally closing in 1957.

Roberts Brothers made hundreds of different products over the lifetime of the company including parlour games, puzzles, card games, dolls and soft toys, children's furniture, toys and crafts. They also made the famous game of Ludo.

Gloucester Railway Carriage & Wagon Company

The Gloucester Wagon Company was set up by a group of local merchants as a joint stock company for the manufacture of railway wagons in 1860. The first sod of the new works was cut by the Chairman of the Company, Richard Potter, on 10 April. A sealed bottle, containing coins of the period and parchment inscribed with the names of the directors and General Manager, was placed beneath the first stone of the workshops. The company benefitted from being on the banks of the Gloucester and Berkeley Canal within easy reach of the ports of Sharpness and Bristol and close to the coalfields of the Forest of Dean, the West Midlands and South Wales. Its 5-acre site was served by the Midland Railway High Orchard Branch. Despite a slight lull in production in 1862 due to the American Civil War the company produced Britain's first all-iron goods wagon, known as an 8 ton open. In 1867, they gained their first overseas order for 500 sets of wagon ironwork for the Great Indian Peninsular Railway. The second foreign order, for carriages, came from the Buenos Aires Great Southern Railway of Argentina and the first home order for carriages came from the London Chatham & Dover Railway.

A plaque of the Gloucester Railway Carriage & Wagon Company on display at the West Australian Railway Museum in Perth, Australia. C. C. Hugh Llewellyn.

The company developed a long business relationship in 1868 with Tsarist Russia. The Orel & Vitebsk Railway was their first customer with an order worth £230,000. Apparently, a special axle grease had to be specified for this customer, as the regular grease was found to be poisonous when eaten by starving Russian peasants.

In 1888 the company changed its name to the Gloucester Railway Carriage and Wagon Company. The company continued to operate, with a number of changes, through to the sixties when in 1961 the Gloucester Railway Carriage and Wagon Company was acquired by Winget of Rochester in Kent. The new parent company was called Winget Gloucester Ltd The Wagon Works Sports and Social Club in Tuffley Avenue, known locally as The Winget, is still in existence today. It was set up originally as a social club for workers and their families.

Fielding & Platt

For over a century Fielding & Platt operated their engineering firm in Gloucester and became one of the most innovative and successful engineering companies in the world. Based in the old Atlas Iron Works at Gloucester Docks, Fielding & Platt, was Gloucester's finest engineering company. They achieved worldwide importance for manufacturing a range of machinery and plant that was to change working practices in a number of important areas such as locomotive manufacture and ship building. It also gained a reputation for the longevity and reliability of its products. They built the bridge across the river Severn by the North Warehouse at Gloucester Docks. Constructed in 1880, this bridge was only replaced in 1962, such longevity being the trademark of Fielding & Platt products.

The company was founded in October 1866 by Samuel Fielding and James Platt who combined their engineering skills and business acumen. In 1868 they produced the first Gloucester built iron sea-going steamer, followed in 1874 by a small steam boat, the SS *Sabrina*, built for the Gloucester Dock Company. From 1871 the company began to specialize in hydraulic engineering, for in that year, a skilled and innovative engineer, Ralph Hart Tweddel approached the partnership with plans for a portable riveter he had invented. The partners backed the project, going on to develop a range of portable riveters based on the Tweddel System. Such was the success of the riveter, that before long it had been widely adopted by the shipbuilding industry and was in use throughout much of the world as far as Sydney Australia when it was used in the construction of the Sydney Harbour Bridge.

Following Samuel Fielding's death in 1874, his two sons joined the business. The company continued to grow and patented many of their products.

In 1882, the company developed a two stroke engine that was powered by town gas and fitted with electrical ignition. A few years later came the four stroke variants with tube ignition. Later refinements included a semi-diesel engine, followed in 1912 by the first patented heavy-oil engine. By the 1920s, they had introduced the Cold Start Engine but their mainstay continued to be in hydraulic engineering. Several notable examples included the overhead gantries installed at the Harland & Wolff Shipyard in Belfast and the installation of the hydraulic lifts in Blackpool Tower in 1898.

Fielding & Platt were responsible for producing the first vacuum cleaners in Britain based on Hugh Cecil Booth's design. As a result, the British Vacuum Cleaner Company was formed.

The complex engineering of what was a scrap metal baling plant at the Fielding & Platt factory.

During the First World War, the company started the production of extrusion presses which remained one of the company's principal specialties. Other machinery for the war effort included specialised shell banding presses, hydraulic systems for tank assembly factories, gun sight mechanisms, and a thousand sets of mine sinkers, as well as the hydraulic launching gear for HMS *Achilles, Thunderer* and *Orion*.

During the Second World War, the company manufactured a 4,000 ton press for the Bristol Aeroplane Company, used for the production of aircraft components and a similar press for Fairey Aviation Ltd. They also built a stretch-forming press for the manufacture of the leading edges of Spitfire and Hurricane wings, plus a 4,700 ton press for making laminated wooden propellers. Throughout both wars the company made heading presses for the manufacture of shell case ends, and drawing and capping plant for making shell cases.

During the '80s the business went through a series of redundancies and restructuring and sadly, in 2003, Fielding and Platt closed down what remained of the Gloucester operation, which ended centuries of engineering brilliance.

Hubert Cecil Booth, 1871–1955

Booth was born in Theresa Place, Gloucester before moving at age nine to Belle Vue House in Spa Road. He attended the County Primary School in Hempsted and went on to be educated at King's School.

In 1900 Booth saw a demonstration of a compressed air-based cleaning system for railway carriages at St Pancras station. Booth reasoned that sucking air through a filter might be a better system, and thus invented an early version of the domestic vacuum cleaner. which was manufactured by Fielding & Platt of Gloucester. In 1902 he founded the British Vacuum Cleaner and Engineering Company. He also designed suspension bridges and factories and like Fielding and Platt, who also worked on Blackpool Tower, Booth designed the famous Ferris Wheel in Blackpool which opened to the public in 1896.

Matchmaking

S. J. Moreland & Sons

Samuel John Moreland, originally from Stroud, established the famous matchmaking business in 1867, making Lucifer and Vesta matches. The company took advantage of new forms of phosphorus and the new formulas, which removed the dangerous element in both match making and match using, and which brought in the era of the safety match.

England's Glory, with the dreadnought, HMS *Devastation* was the firm's most famous brand of matches and became a household name. They were early pioneers in the field of sales promotion with their consumer competitions and gift schemes and introduced various efficiencies such as the purchase of the first delivery lorry to replace horse-drawn transport and the introduction of the first continuous automatic match making machinery.

His two sons, Philip and Harry, assisted him in the business until, at the age of ninety-six, he died. He was said to be a vigorous employer, tough and strong-willed but also fair-minded, dedicated to the interests of his factory and its people. At the time of his death the *Gloucester Journal* stated, 'He deserves to be remembered with the greatest respect and gratitude as one of the makers of modern Gloucester. ... Mr. Moreland is the last of a band of contemporaries to whose memory the citizens can never be sufficiently grateful.'

The company was then led by his son Harry, who also displayed a single-minded devotion to matchmaking. The works committee minutes of 16 September 1954 record this reference by his son, Henry. 'I doubt whether anyone, at any time, in our industry, in any part of the world, has devoted himself with such singleness of purpose or with greater determination and ability.' Henry, the third generation of Moreland, took over his father's work and launched a major re-organisation of the layout of the manufacturing departments and introduced a wide range of measures to improve the welfare and working conditions of the employees. In 1961, Henry Moreland retired, and handed over the running of the firm to his two sons, Samuel John Moreland and Robert Moreland.

At the time of the Crimean War, S. J. Moreland were making wooden hospital huts and during the First World War they revived the old kelp industry which made chlorate of potash, an essential ingredient in match making, which was at that time almost exclusively a German product. In the Second World War they made striker sticks for bombs and did the finishing work on waterproof match containers. At the request of the government, a proportion of Moreland's boxes carried war effort slogans, such as Save Fuel for Battle, in the space normally occupied by their jokes.

In 1913 they were taken over by the match makers, Bryant and May. In 1919 they erected new factory buildings on the corner of Bristol and Stroud Road which still stands today, along with the iconic image of a lighted match, the trade mark of S. J. Moreland.

Waterways in Gloucester

The river Severn, at 220 miles, is the longest river in the United Kingdom. In Gloucester, it has long been a waterway of strategic importance. The Romans knew it as *Sabrina Fluvius*, the Welsh as Hafren and the English as the Severn. The river's estuary, which empties into the Bristol Channel, has the second largest tidal range in the world at 48 feet and, of course, is famous for the unique and curious phenomena of the Severn Bore. Since the arrival of the Romans the River Severn has played a strategically important role as it was the lowest bridging point of the river and thus controlled the main route into Wales from southern England.

Above: Surfers on the unique and natural phenomenon which is the Severn Bore.

Left: The iconic image of the S. J. Moreland brand. It is still to be found on the corner of the Moreland's factory in the Bristol Road.

The Gloucester Trow

A Trow was a shallow draft, sailing vessel with an open hold and a square rig. It was used to transport goods along the River Severn as early as medieval times because of its usefulness in shallow waters and the ability to lower its masts when navigating low bridges.

The Cotswold Canals Trust logo features a Gloucester Trow taken from a token, issued locally when there was a national shortage of small change, dating from 1790s.

The only surviving complete Severn trow, is the Spry, which was built by William Hurd of Chepstow in 1894. It was registered at Gloucester on 25 October of that year and her first owner was William Davis, a Chepstow stone merchant.

The Old Custom House

In 1580 the city corporation built a custom house in what was then known as the King's Quay, also known as Dockham Ditch. Part of the building was used as a warehouse and by 1630 the customs officers occupied the upper rooms and the corporation kept its stock of coal for sale to the poor at low prices in the warehouse underneath. The fuel was dispensed from a penthouse, a shed or standing attached to the front of the building, which by 1636 was known as Pennyless Bench. In 1724 the custom office was enlarged by carrying the two storeys above the warehouse forwards on pillars which can still be seen today and give the building its characteristic look. This was built over the site of Pennyless Bench. The new building was faced in ashlar and decorated with pilasters and a cornice. John Pitt, the then Collector of the Customs, purchased the building in 1799.

Gloucester & Berkeley Canal Company

In 1793 industrialists, merchants and other influential residents of Gloucester obtained an Act of Parliament to construct a ship canal between Gloucester and Berkeley to bypass a treacherous stretch of the River Severn. Sea-going ships would be able to reach Gloucester and the hope was that in time it would rival the port of Bristol in importance. The project encountered many difficulties and it wasn't until 1827 that the canal was completed. In its day, the Gloucester & Sharpness Canal was once the broadest and deepest in the world. Thomas Telford, the noted canal and bridge builder, was the engineering advisor and acted as consultant to the canal company.

Chandlery

Messrs. Johns & Sons

Based at No. 21 Commercial Road in Gloucester Messrs Johns & Sons were Ship Chandlers, Sail Makers and General Merchants and were one of the oldest firms in Gloucester.

The Docks

The development of the canal system gave rise to the construction of several large warehouses and a dry dock at Gloucester. They were built as bonded warehouses for wealthy corn merchants, millers, maltsters and timber merchants. They were mainly designed by local architect, John Jacques and built by local builder, Joseph Moss. Most of these warehouses have found alternative uses, either as offices, restaurants, pubs or museums.

The Waterways Museum

Llanthony Warehouse was built in 1873 by Capel N. Tripp, a local architect for corn merchants Wait James & Company. It was converted in 1987 as the National Waterways Museum for the British Waterways Board.

Painted in 1908 by John Pockett, this oil on canvas is of *The Spry*, a Severn Trow, seen here in the Severn Estuary, sloop rigged, with the islands of Flat and Steep Holm in the background.

DID YOU KNOW THAT...?

Howard Blackburn (1859–1932) was an American fisherman who on Saturday 19 August 1899 sailed into Gloucester Docks having just completed an epic single-handed voyage across the Atlantic from our name-sake town Gloucester in Massachusetts. Blackburn had set sail on Sunday 18 June 1899 in his 30-foot vessel *Great Western*. This achievement was made all the more spectacular as Blackburn had lost most of his fingers and toes, including the top joint of his thumbs to frostbite. Sixty-one days after leaving the New England fishing port, Blackburn arrived in Kingroad. After spending Friday night at anchor he took on board a pilot named Frank Price before the short journey to Sharpness, arriving with the afternoon tide. Being part of the Port of Gloucester, under the Queen Elizabeth I charter, the Sharpness Dock Master, hoisted signal flags at the pier head that read Welcome to Gloucester. There was no official reception from the city, but local Sharpness officials were on hand to welcome Blackburn. The SS *Sabrina* happened to be in the port at the time and offered Blackburn a tow along the canal to Gloucester, where a spectacular reception awaited.

The heroic Howard Blackburn, an American fisherman who sailed, singlehandedly across the Atlantic, into Gloucester Docks in 1899.

4. Military Gloucester

The Gloucestershire Regiment

The Gloucestershire Regiment was an infantry regiment of the British Army. Nicknamed The Glorious Glosters, the regiment carried more battle honours on their regimental colours than any other British Army line regiment. Soldiers of the Gloucestershire Regiment, and subsequently the Royal Gloucestershire, Berkshire and Wiltshire Regiment from 1994 onwards, wore a cap badge on both the front and the rear of their headdress, a tradition maintained by soldiers in The Rifles when in service dress. The back badge is unique in the British Army and was adopted by the 28th Regiment of Foot to commemorate their actions at the Battle of Alexandria in 1801. The Gloucestershire Regiment, existed from 1881 until 1994 when it was amalgamated with the Duke of Edinburgh's Royal Regiment to form the Royal Gloucestershire, Berkshire and Wiltshire Regiment which was also merged with several other regiments to create The Rifles.

A tapestry dedicated to the regiment can be found in St Mary de Crypt church. It depicts much of the regiment's history from 1694 onwards.

Sphinx

A pivotal battle in Gloucester's military history took place in 1801 to the east of Alexandria. It was a victory which restored the standing of the British Army in the eyes of their nation and allowed the 28th Regiment (the Gloucestershire Regiment), to wear a sphinx on the rear of their headdress.

The Soldiers of Gloucestershire Museum

Housed in the new Customs House is the Soldiers of Gloucestershire Museum. It was built in 1845 by Sydney Smirke, for the Customs Commissioners to handle the great expansion of foreign trade passing through Gloucester Docks in the second half of the nineteenth century.

The War Memorials

Gloucester Park War Memorial

The war memorial in Gloucester Park was first unveiled at a ceremony in 1925 attended by the Bishop of Gloucester and by the distinguished, senior British Army officer of the First World War, Hubert Plumer. The original memorial was a tapering stone column with a level top which was surmounted by a bust of the Sphinx, an emblem of the Gloucestershire Regiment. In 1933, the council added a curved wall incorporating a series of bronze plaques recording the names of those from the city of Gloucester who are known to have died in the First World War. It now includes the names of those who died in the Second World War and the Korean War.

Above: The city's coat of arms on top of the Regiments of Gloucester Museum, which was once the Customs House in Gloucester Docks.

Left: The War Memorial in Gloucester Park. You can make out the sphinx on top of the tall obelisk.

War Memorial to the Royal Gloucestershire Hussars Yeomanry

This war memorial was unveiled in College Green in 1922. Built by Cash and Wright, with cast bronze bas-relief panels by Adrian Jones, it features a tall cross on a high octagonal plinth in the centre of a wider octagonal base or podium surrounded by three steps. There is a bronze panel on each face of the plinth with four of the panels in bas-relief, each depicting a scene of soldiers of the regiment who served during the First World War in the following campaigns as inscribed on the monument: Sinai 1916, Palestine 1917, Gallipoli 1915, Syria 1918.

The names of the fallen are inscribed on the alternating panels.

The First World War Memorial Plaque at St Michael's Tower

Outside St Michael's Tower is a First World War memorial plaque. It bears some well-known local family names.

First World War Memorial for S. J. Moreland & Sons

A memorial plaque, on the exterior wall of St Stephen's Church in Bristol Road, is dedicated to the employees of the firm. It lists those who enlisted and those who made the supreme sacrifice in the First World War.

Daphne Tank

In 2013 the discovery of a serial number, 2743, on a tank which had been housed in a museum in Lincoln showed that the tank, a First World War, Mark IV female tank was, in fact, from Gloucester. Research has shown that the tank, known as *Daphne*, saw service in France at Passchendaele during the First World War with 12th Company, D. Battalion of the Tank Corps in August 1917. After the war, *Daphne* was shipped back to England and given to the people of Gloucester as a 'Presentation Tank' as a way of honouring the dead and saying thank you. It stood in Gloucester Park from 1919 until the 1940s. She was then on display at Hucclecote Airfield until the end of the Second World War and later arrived at the Royal Armoured Corps Centre at Bovington Camp, Dorset, where she became one of the first exhibits of the Tank Museum.

The Siege of Gloucester

In 1642 civil war broke out in England. Gloucester, a largely Puritan trading city burdened by the illegal taxes of King Charles I, stood against him and sided with the forces of parliament. By 1643 Gloucester stood alone against the King in the west of England, and on 10 August a Royalist army of 30,000 men led by King Charles besieged the city. His opponent was a twenty-three year old Lieutenant Colonel Edward Massie who, as commander of the Gloucester garrison, had just over 1,500 men under him. Despite this, the reinforced medieval walls of Gloucester withstood the King's artillery bombardment for twenty-six days until a relieving parliamentary army arrived from London. Massie had been a professional soldier and military engineer both on the continent and in Scotland before the civil war. In 1660 Massie was elected Member of Parliament for Gloucester. Later, in the reign of Charles II he was knighted and made Governor of Jamaica. The Old Crown Inn on Westgate Street was said to be used by Massie as the siege headquarters.

Gloucester Day

When the citizens of Gloucester rebuilt the South Gate they placed an inscription on the outside reading 'A City Assaulted by Man but Saved by God' and on the inside was a reminder to 'Ever Remember the Fifth of September 1643, Give God the Glory.' This date is still celebrated today on what has become officially known as Gloucester Day.

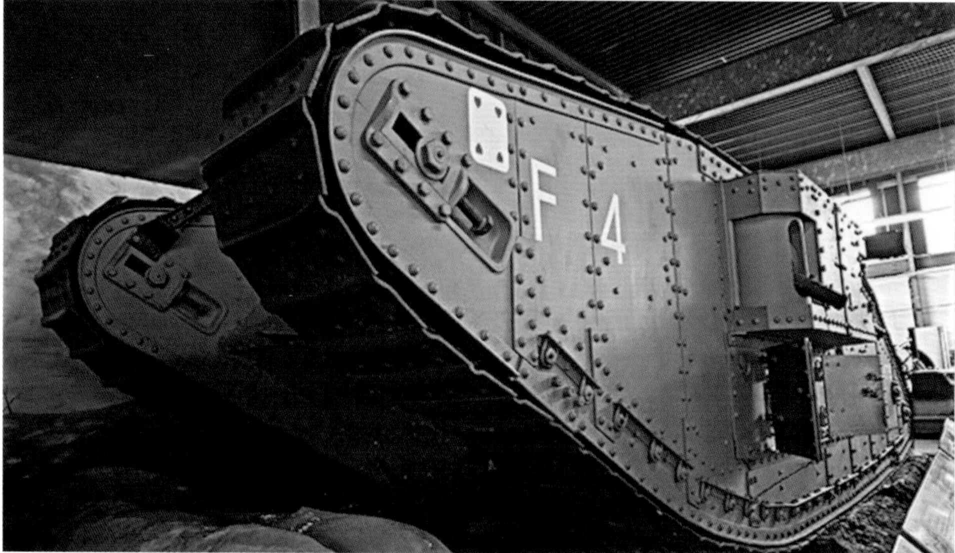

Top left: The First World War memorial dedicated solely to the workers of S. J. Moreland on the outside wall of St Stephen's church on the Bristol Road.

Top Right: The young twenty-three-year-old Lieutenant Colonel Edward Massie who defended the city from the Royalists in the Siege of Gloucester during the Civil War in 1643.

Above: The female *Daphne* Tank, Serial Number 2743, Mark IV, given to the people of Gloucester after the war to say thank you, on display at the Museum of Lincolnshire Life.

DID YOU KNOW THAT...?

There has been a suggestion that Humpty Dumpty was a 'tortoise' siege engine, an armoured frame, used unsuccessfully to approach the walls of the Parliamentary-held city of Gloucester in 1643 during the Siege of Gloucester in the English Civil War. This theory was put forward in 1956 by Professor David Daube in *The Oxford* magazine on the basis of a contemporary account of the attack, but without evidence that the rhyme was connected. Nevertheless, it is a popular theory in Gloucester!

Left: The original South Gate, with its timber latticework structure, was removed in the seventeenth century and is now on display in the Folk Museum.

Right: Tucked away, at the end of an obscure lane, just off Three Cocks Lane, is the unloved statue of Charles II.

The Mock Mayor of Barton Parade

When Charles II returned to the throne in 1660, following the English Civil War, he punished Gloucester for supporting Cromwell by reducing the city's boundaries. This left the parish of Barton outside the city and not under the control of the Mayor of Gloucester. Barton elected a 'mock mayor' to poke fun at the city. This tradition has been revived in recent years and the annual parade is led by the real Mayor and Sheriff of Gloucester, complete with Mock Mayor and Town Crier.

King Charles II, 1630–1685

Hidden away at the end of an obscure dead end just off Three Cocks Lane is the unremarkable statue of King Charles II, carved from limestone in 1662 by Stephen Baldwyn, a local carver. Being in a quite weathered and uncared for state, some would argue it is just deserts for a king who punished the city following the siege of Gloucester. Described as a slightly larger than life standing figure, crowned and wearing royal robes, it was originally set within a niche at the north end of the Wheat Market House in the middle of Southgate Street and is thought to have been removed circa 1785.

In 1960 a plaque was placed on the front of it, inscribed:

> CHARLES II. This statue was carved in 1662 by Stephen Baldwyn and was set up in the Wheat Market in Southgate Street. It was removed in the middle of the eighteenth century and its whereabouts remained obscure until 1945 when it was rediscovered in pieces at Chex Hill. Re-erected in this position in 1960.

Gloster Aircraft Company

The Gloster Aircraft Company was founded in 1917 and, during its heyday, it produced 12,500 aircraft of forty-eight different types, including the E28/39, Britain's and the Allies' first jet aircraft. In 1925, a gifted engineer, George Carter, who lived in Dog Lane, Crickley Hill overlooking the Brockworth aerodrome, had joined the company and by 1930 he was working in new premises in Hucclecote. Then in 1939, Carter was asked by the Air Ministry to submit plans for a brand-new aeroplane built around Frank Whittle's engine. The new aeroplane, the *E28/39*, took only 15 months to build, much of the assembly being built in secret at the Regents Garage in Cheltenham.

On 8 April 1941, the plane had its maiden flight at Hucclecote. Although its engine was the brainchild of Frank, later to become, Sir Frank Whittle inventor of the jet engine, the aeroplane itself had been designed by George Carter. However, it was his *F18/37* proposal that attracted the attention of Frank Whittle as a possible airframe for his revolutionary new gas turbine.

George Carter was awarded the CBE in 1947 and appointed Technical Director of the Gloster Aircraft Company in 1948. He remained on the board of directors until 1948.

By the time the company closed down it had provided employment for some 20,000 Gloucester people and become famous for designing and building planes with names such as The *Gloster Meteor, Javelin* and *Gladiator.*

Jet Age Museum

The jet engine was designed by British engineering genius Sir Frank Whittle (1907–1996). His son Ian is now a patron of the Jet Age Museum in Staverton. Many of the aeroplanes designed by George Carter are on display. The original jet engine aeroplane can be seen in London's Science Museum. A full-size replica is proudly on display at the Jet Age Museum, built by volunteers.

Aviation Gardens

This garden was created to honour Gloucester's servicemen and can be found close to Gloucester City Museum. It once contained murals dedicated to the Gloster Aircraft Company. These can now be viewed at the Jet Age Museum in Staverton.

The commemorative plaque on the very site where the first jet engine took flight, at Hucclecote in Gloucester.

5. Notable Gloucestrians

Gloucester has been blessed with an abundance of talented and memorable characters over the millenia. May it continue.

John Taylor, 1578–1653

John Taylor was an English poet who dubbed himself 'The Water Poet' or the 'King's Water Poet'. Born in Gloucester in 1578, the son of a surgeon, he was educated at Crypt grammar school and became, as he said, 'mired in Latin accidence'. As a young boy he was apprenticed to a Thames boatman. After his waterman apprenticeship he served in Essex's fleet, and was present at Flores in 1597 and at the siege of Cadiz.

Among his many accomplishments Taylor is one of the few early authors of a palindrome. In 1614, he wrote, 'Lewd did I live, & evil I did dwel.' He also wrote a poem about Thomas Parr, a man who supposedly lived to the age of 152 and constructed a language called Barmoodan.

He achieved notoriety by a series of eccentric journeys. On one such journey he travelled from London to Queenborough in Kent in a paper boat with two stockfish tied to canes for oars. He described this jourey in *The Praise of Hemp-Seed*, which was re-enacted in 2006.

Many of Taylor's works were published by subscription. He would propose a book, ask for contributors, and write it when he had enough subscribers to undertake the printing costs. He had more than 1,600 subscribers to *The Pennylesse Pilgrimage* or 'The Moneylesse Perambulation of John Taylor, alias the Kings Magesties Water-Poet; How he Travailed on Foot from London to Edenborough in Scotland, Not Carrying any Money to or fro, Neither Begging, Borrowing, or Asking Meate, Drinke, or Lodging', which he published in 1618. Those who defaulted on their subscription were chided the following year in a scathing brochure entitled A Kicksey Winsey, or, A Lerry Come-Twang, which he issued in the following year.

John Ricketts I, 1691–1734

John Ricketts arrived in Gloucester in 1710. In that same year he petitioned the city corporation to be made a Freeman of the City, offering in return to execute a statue in stone of Queen Anne. The proposal was accepted and he became a Freeman on 11 September 1711. In 1712 he received a part-payment of £23 for the statue. George Vertue, engraver and Fellow of the Society of Antiquaries visited Gloucester in 1729 and noted, 'Mr ... Rickett Stone Carver. At Glocestr a Son-a hopeful young man ...'

Ricketts appears to have worked on a considerable amount of stone carving in the city and surrounding district, including the wall monument to William Lisle in Gloucester Cathedral, which has a convincing portrait bust in wig and contemporary dress, set in

An engraving of the self-styled Water Poet, one of Gloucester's most bizarre and fascinating figures of the seventeenth century.

an elaborate architectural surround. John Ricketts died in 1734, leaving six children, including two sons, Thomas and William.

Thomas Ricketts, who was his father's executor, took on the business and lived in Eastgate Street. He was responsible for a number of elegant, crisply-carved wall-monuments, for instance the memorial to Lady Strachan, which has a convincing portrait medallion held by a grieving putto. He died on 20 June 1780 and was buried with his wife, Martha who died before him in 1773 in St Michael's church on The Cross. Thomas was responsible for the wall monument erected in the portico of The Boothall, which now resides on a wall in Three Cocks Lane. The date of this work is unknown. The 1750 drawing of The High Cross is also by Thomas Ricketts.

Thomas's son, John Ricketts II, was baptised at St Michael's church in 1740. One of his finest monuments, to Elizabeth Charlett, has a lively portrait bust above a sarcophagus. In addition to his work as a sculptor, he was busily engaged in building work in Gloucester for some years and frequent mention is made of him in the corporation Minutes. In 1778 he submitted a proposal with a ground plan to the corporation for demolishing Eastgate and adjoining buildings. He appears to have been successful, for documents in private hands are said to show that he built and presumably designed Eastgate House in Gloucester, *c.* 1780. Eastgate House has been described as 'an Adamish stone-fronted' building demolished when the King's Walk Shopping Centre was developed. Ricketts appears to have designed the triumphal arch erected in Gloucester in 1777 in honour of William Bromley Chester, MP for that city. An engraving of the arch in the Gloucester Folk Museum is signed 'John Ricketts, Statuary at Gloucester'. In 1784 Ricketts was among those who surveyed the tower of St Nicholas church, receiving £1 11*s* 6*d* for his plan. He died in 1796 leaving a son, Thomas, who joined the family firm.

James Wood, 1756–1836

James Wood was the grandson of the founder of the Gloucester Old Bank, probably born above No. 22 Westgate Street, the business premises of his family's bank. He was baptised at St Nicholas' Church in Westgate Street and may have attended Sir Thomas Rich's School in Eastgate Street. He inherited the family business, which included the bank and a drapery business from his grandfather, also called James Wood, in 1802. He became known, locally, as 'Jemmy' Wood. The whole bank was believed to have consisted of just Jemmy and two clerks. On the counter were nailed counterfeit coins as a warning to customers not to try and pass them off on the bank. Jemmy's practice was to offer no interest on deposits of less than one year. He served as Sheriff of Gloucester in 1811 and 1813 and also served as an Alderman from 1820 until his death. It was said he could have served as the city's Mayor but never held the post due, apparently, to the expense of holding the office.

Despite his increasing prosperity and national fame, he became a target of caricaturists not only as a result of his well-known miserliness but also from his shabby appearance. His profile was said to be 'of protruding chin and nose, and sloping forehead'. His miserliness and wealth brought him national fame when a Staffordshire figure, based upon him, was created for a Toby Jug.

Jemmy was buried in St Mary De Crypt Church in Southgate Street and left an estate valued at £900,000, most of which was consumed by legal arguments over his will. The Gloucester Old Bank was absorbed by the County of Gloucestershire Banking Company in 1838, which in turn was taken over by Lloyds Bank in 1897.

Problems over his will led to a long court case that soaked up much of the funds in the estate. He never married and had no children. He left over £1 million, at today's prices, to

A miniature of Jemmy Wood by an unknown artist.

be shared equally between Sir Matthew Wood, John Chadborn, Jacob Osborne and John S. Surman, who were his executors. A damaged codicil was found that left money to the City of Gloucester and to other beneficiaries and it was the wrangling over the authenticity of this codicil that caused the settlement of the estate to be delayed.

Three years after his death John Chadborn, who had been cited as an executor of Jemmy's will, killed himself. The entry in *The Gentleman's Magazine* of 1839, in itself, reads like an excerpt from *Bleak House*:

> 6 August. At Gloucester, aged about fifty-five, Mr John Chadborn, solicitor, the executor and residuary legatee under the will of the late Mr James Wood, the wealthy banker and shopkeeper, since whose death his attention has been almost wholly engrossed with the proceedings consequent upon the disputed validity of the will. About eight o' clock in the morning, the body of Mr Chadborn was found suspended by a rope; life had been extinct some time. Verdict: Temporary Insanity. He has left a widow and two married daughters.

Mary Elizabeth Fluck, 1857–1927

Miss Fluck was an early Gloucester feminist, setting up a charity and convalescent home to support women who had fallen on bad times in the city. She was born in Tewkesbury to Richard Fluck who was a corn merchant trading in Gloucester. At the age of twenty-three Miss Fluck moved to Winslow in Buckinghamshire to be a governess at an all girl's boarding school. By 1901 she was back living with her parents and brothers in The Limes in Longford. Following the death of her brother John in 1926, she inherited £160,000. By the following September, in 1927, Miss Fluck she died whilst visiting Whitby. She remained a spinster until her death at the age of seventy. By this time she was living in Malvern House in Denmark Road. She seemed to have spent a good deal of her inheritance leaving only £25,500 in her will. She did bequeath and endow her family home, The Limes in Longford, as a Convalescent Home for women and children. She is buried with her brother in Twigworth parish church.

In 1940 the corporation requisitioned and fitted the Fluck convalescent home as a temporary maternity hospital while it built Gloucester Maternity Hospital. By the

DID YOU KNOW THAT...?

Charles Dickens took inspiration from Gloucester's own legendary miser, Jemmy Wood, for the main character of Ebeneezer Scrooge in *A Christmas Carol.* It has also been suggested that the interminable court case of Jarndyce vs Jarndyce in Dickens' *Bleak House* may have been based on that which arose following irregularities in Wood's will, absorbing most of his estate. A character by the name of Dismal Jemmy appears in *The Pickwick Papers* and Jemmy Wood of Gloucester is also mentioned in *Our Mutual Friend.*

The gravestone, erected in Twigworth Parish church, to the memory of Mary Elizabeth Fluck, an early Gloucester feminist and benefactor.

mid-1940s the Fluck convalescent home was used by the corporation as a children's home.

The Fluck Convalescent Fund still operates today and remains a charity handing out grants to women of all ages and children under sixteen who live in the city of Gloucester and its surrounding area, and who are in poor health or convalescing after illness or operative treatment. In 1971 the Fluck Convalescent Fund had an income of £3,600. In 2011 the Fund had given over £29,000 in grants to needy women and children and had at least £500,000 more on account.

Charles Wheatstone, 1802–1875

Charles Wheatstone was born in Barnwood, Gloucester. He was the son of a shoemaker whose wider family had connections to the music business, being musical instrument makers and dealers. In 1806 the family moved to London and in 1816 at the age of fourteen he became apprenticed to his uncle, an instrument maker. Aged only sixteen he produced his first new musical instrument, the flute harmonique, and went on to design and patent a number of other instruments, including the concertina. He quickly became fascinated by the wonders of sound and its transmission, publishing his first paper on his experiments as early as 1823. Before long, Wheatstone began to make his name with various inventions. One, which he later perfected, was the bellows-blown English concertina still in use today, and still made by the firm of Wheatstone & Co. This was an area in which he remained interested for the rest of his life. Wheatstone later became interested in optics. His research led to the invention of the stereoscope, which demonstrated how pictures could be visually combined to create the illusion of depth.

Wheatstone is best known for his invention of an electric telegraph however, he invented and contributed in several fields of science, including photography, electrical generators, encryption, and acoustics and music. Wheatstone had a lifelong friendship with the physicist Michael Faraday, who delivered Wheatstone's lectures on sound and acoustics at the Royal Institution. Wheatstone won many awards, including several in France, and was elected a Fellow of the Royal Society in 1836. He died in Paris in 1875.

Thomas Gambier Parry, 1816–1888

Thomas was an English artist and art collector. He is best remembered for his development of the Gambier Parry process of fresco painting. He moved to Highnam Court, Gloucestershire when he was twenty-one. After studying the technique of the Italian fresco painters, Thomas Gambier Parry invented the Spirit Fresco, a process of mural painting appropriate for the damp English climate which he used in his private chapel at Highnam. He also executed grand-scale mural projects at Gloucester Cathedral. He founded the Gloucester Science and Art Society. Thomas Gambier Parry was a notable collector of medieval and Renaissance art. In 1966, the Courtauld Institute was bequeathed his collection.

William Ernest Henley, 1849–1903

Henley was an English poet, critic and editor, best remembered for his 1875 poem 'Invictus'. Henley was born in Gloucester and was the oldest of a family of six children, five sons and a daughter. His father, William, was a struggling bookseller and stationer.

Between 1861 and 1867, Henley was a pupil at The Crypt School in Gloucester. At age twelve he was diagnosed with tubercular arthritis which necessitated the amputation of one of his legs just below the knee; the other foot was saved only through radical surgery performed by Joseph Lister in Edinburgh. As he healed in the infirmary, Henley began to write poems, including the influential poem 'Invictus'. The poem has informed popular culture ever since.

Henley's sickly young daughter, Margaret Henley, was immortalized by J. M. Barrie in his children's classic, Peter Pan. Unable to speak clearly, young Margaret had called her friend Barrie her 'fwendy-wendy', resulting in the use of 'Wendy' in the book. Margaret did not survive long enough to read the book; she died on 11 February 1894 at the age of five.

DID YOU KNOW THAT...?

In the 1942 film *Casablanca,* Captain Renault, an official played by Claude Rains recites the last two lines of the poem 'Invictus' when talking to Rick Blaine, played by Humphrey Bogart, referring to his power in Casablanca. The line 'bloody, but unbowed' was the *Daily Mirror*'s headline the day after the 7 July 2005 London bombings. The poem's last stanza was quoted by US President Barack Obama at the end of his speech at Nelson Mandela's memorial service on 10 December 2013 in South Africa and published on the front cover of the December 2013 issue of *The Economist.*

Henley died of tuberculosis in 1903 at the age of fifty-three at his home in Woking, and, after cremation at the local crematorium his ashes were interred in his daughter, Margaret's grave. At age 12 Henley was diagnosed with tubercular arthritis that necessitated the amputation of one of his legs just below the knee; the other foot was saved only through a radical surgery performed by Joseph Lister. As he healed in the infirmary, Henley began to write poems, including "Invictus,"

F. W. Harvey DCM, 1888–1957

Frederick William Harvey was an English poet, broadcaster and solicitor whose poetry became popular during and after the First World War. He was later known as the 'Laureate of Gloucestershire'. Born in Hartpury, he was educated at King's School, Gloucester, where he formed a close friendship with Ivor Gurney. Gurney and Herbert Howells, another local composer, would set a number of his poems to music.

In 1914 he joined the 5th battalion of the Gloucestershire Regiment as a private and was later awarded a Distinguished Conduct Medal for conspicuous gallantry. His most prolific writing period came when he was a prisoner of war. His poem 'In Flanders' deals with his homesickness for Gloucestershire and was said to have been composed after climbing Robinswood Hill. His friend Ivor Gurney, writing about his musical score for Harvey's poem, wrote in a letter to Marion Scott in 1916: 'As for "In Flanders"... I'm glad he went to Robinswood Hill; the view from there is magnificent. Do you know, standing off from

A bronze bust, by the famous sculptor, Auguste Rodin, of William Ernest Henley.

my song, I can now see that the very spirit of my county is quick in the song. Gloster itself shines and speaks in it.'

In 2012 the F. W. Harvey Society collaborated with Gloucestershire Archives to produce a comprehensive online catalogue of a vast amount of unpublished material, more than several thousand separate items.

Harvey was commemorated by a slate memorial tablet in the south transept of Gloucester Cathedral in 1980.

DID YOU KNOW THAT...?

According to Robert Louis Stevenson's letters, the idea for the character of Long John Silver was inspired by his real-life friend Henley. In a letter to Henley after the publication of *Treasure Island*, Stevenson wrote, 'I will now make a confession: It was the sight of your maimed strength and masterfulness that begot Long John Silver ... the idea of the maimed man, ruling and dreaded by the sound, was entirely taken from you.'

6. Treasures of Gloucester

Gloucester possesses many treasures. Most can be seen in the city's museums or around the city's streets. Many artefacts stored in its museums have been found by accident, others uncovered during the many archaeological digs that have taken place over the years in the city. Here are a selection of some of my favourites.

The Gloucester Candlestick

This candlestick dates from between 1104 and 1113. It originally belonged to the Abbey of St Peter, now Gloucester Cathedral, but somehow ended up in the treasury of Le Mans Cathedral. It is now on display in the Victoria and Albert Museum in London. As such metalwork was commonly melted down and reused, its survival is both remarkable and significant, showcasing techniques and craftsmanship in the Romanesque style which might otherwise have been lost. Even more exceptional are the three Latin inscriptions that reveal the candlestick's history, meaning and provenance.

The inscription around the stem reads, 'The devotion of Abbot Peter and his gentle flock gave me to the Church of St Peter of Gloucester'. Peter was the abbot of the Benedictine Abbey of St Peter between 1104 and 1113, which is why the candlestick is dated to this period. Abbot Peter continued the programme of building and expansion begun by Abbot Serlo in about 1072, progressing the building of St Peter's Church. The donation of a rich gift such as this candlestick marked the wealth and success of the Benedictine community.

The inscription around the outside of the drip pan reads, 'Burden of light, work of virtue, brilliantly shining teaching preaches so that Man may not be darkened by sin.' This suggests the candlestick may have symbolised the light which illuminated virtue of Christian teaching and prevented the shadow of sin. In practical terms it may have been used on the altar or to light a shrine.

The Gloucester Candlestick is decorated with a menagerie of real and fantastic creatures. Winged dragons support the drip pan, apes clamber along the stem and hybrid animals bite, grab and pull for position among foliage and flowers along the base. Among the dragons and beasts, the symbols of the four evangelists can be found at the knop (the ornamental swell in the middle of the stem). The candlestick has often been interpreted as the struggle of vice and virtue, as the creatures strive to reach the light or sink into the darkness below. The decoration is closely related to manuscript illumination, which commonly depicted real and mythological beasts of vibrant colours hidden among, struggling against, or growing as part of, the wild undergrowth. On the Gloucester Candlestick, as in many contemporary illuminations, each creature and foliate spray is connected, creating a sense of ordered chaos. Both speech and silence appear as themes within the decoration. Apes and hybrid creatures are silenced by their neighbours, or are caught whispering to one another. Figures such as apes were associated with sin and the devil in medieval bestiaries, while hybrid creatures such as centaurs were sometimes considered to have no soul. Perhaps the silencing of secretive chatter of these bestial creatures visually expresses the need to listen to the teaching of God. This reinforces the message of the inscription of the drip pan, which says that 'shining doctrine teaches so that man be not shadowed by vice.'

Medieval Graffiti

You probably think that graffiti is a modern activity carried out by youngsters with spray cans. Think again. Medieval graffiti is surprisingly quite common and we have a number of examples here in Gloucester. My particular favourite is to be found in the scriptorium of Blackfriars Priory. Often referred to as The Madonna and Child, it features the face of a woman and that of a small child. The explanation for its existence is that a pious, but bored monk, sat at his study carrel and carved this.

Other examples of medieval graffiti can be found on the outside wall of the Chapel of St Mary Magdalene, the chapel of the former leper hospital in London Road. Thought to have been made by pilgrims, they feature a Star of Epiphany, various crosses and a fleur de lys of the Virgin Mary.

Mosaic Floor

This fourth century Roman mosaic floor was found beneath Debenhams department store in Northgate Street. Part of an elaborate six colour design and thought to measure some 26 feet square, it is now on display in Gloucester City Museum.

Stamped Tile

The Romans had a tilery on the site of St Oswald's Priory. This tile is stamped with the names of the Roman magistrates, Julius Florius and Cornelius Similus who must have worked for the council. The Latin letters RPG, which stands for *res publica glevum* and loosely means Gloucester City Council were also stamped on the tile.

DID YOU KNOW THAT...?

In 1455, Robert Cole, the Canon of Llanthony Secunda, undertook a complete rental survey of all the buildings and tenements in the city. In 1890, W. H. Stevenson edited the manuscript, with a Latin translation. In his book he describes the manuscript: It is in the form of a roll, consisting of twelve membranes of parchment joined one to another by stitches of black silk thread. In length the roll measures thirty three feet, and in breath fourteen and a half inches. It is in good preservation, with the exception of a few lines at the beginning that may have become defaced by the frequent rolling and unrolling of the manuscript. The manuscript is written throughout in a large and bold hand...' This important and historic manuscript is in the careful protection of the Gloucester Records Office.

A picture of the Gloucester Candlestick, on display in the Victoria and Albert Museum, showing the intricate detail and skilled craftsmanship of the piece.

A Star of Epiphany carved into the stone of St Mary Magdalene's Chapel.

A very fine example of medieval graffiti, carved by one of the monks in the scriptorium of Blackfriars Priory.

The well-preserved mosaic floor, showing the design of interlacing cable and plait borders with stylised floral and geometric patterns.

The roman tile found on the site of St Oswald's Priory displaying the names of the Roman magistrates who worked in the city and the Latin lettering RPG denoting the equivalent of today's City Council.

Column

The reception area in Gloucester's City Museum is home to the remains of a wonderful Roman column found in 1971 during the building of Midland Bank (now HSBC) and thought to have been 30 foot high, which supported a large exercise hall. I always marvel at the fact that a Roman stonemason touched this stone but probably didn't hug it – as I am tempted to do every time I see it.

Eastgate Viewing Chamber

Situated in front of Boots the Chemist, on the corner of Eastgate Street and Brunswick Road and below pavement level is this viewing chamber. Most of the Roman and Medieval remains can be seen from street level but it is not until you enter the chamber that you really get the feeling of being back in the past. The chamber contains the remains of a Roman gate post from the first century, a thirteenth-century tower as well as the remains of a sixteenth-century horse pool, used for washing horses before they went to market.

Rufus Sita Tombstone

One of the most significant Roman finds, this almost intact Roman tombstone of oolitic limestone, was found in 1824 outside of the north gate of the Colonia, and near the intersection of London Road and Denmark Road. With only the lower margin

Above: Part of the thirteenth-century tower, thought to have been built in 1230, is just one of the treasures to be found in this underground chamber.

Left: The adorable column, standing proud in the reception area of Gloucester City Museum. For some reason the base of this column is to be found in the window of HSBC bank on the corner of The Cross.

broken off, it features a mounted trooper, with a shield on his left arm and a lance in his right hand with a sheathed sword on his right flank. He rides over a prostrate enemy, who brandishes a short sword in his right hand. Above the relief is a Sphinx, flanked on either side by a lion.

Best Chamber Plaster Decoration

In the timber-framed rear wing of a shoe shop in Westgate Street is a particularly fine example of early-seventeenth-century plaster decoration. The figures over the fireplace depict 'an unusual scene of indigenous peoples of Central America, typical of early

DID YOU KNOW THAT...?

If you walk into the garden of the Dick Whittington pub in Upper Westgate Street you will find the remains of a Roman column tucked away in the corner of the pub garden.

The Rufus Sita tombstone is a rare and almost complete example of a Roman tombstone. Dated between AD 43 and 410, the epitaph reads: 'Rufus Sita, trooper of the Sixth Cohort of Thracians, aged 40, of 22 years' service, lies buried here. His heirs had this erected according to the terms of his will.'

seventeenth- century engravings, with stiff feather headdresses and skirts showing bounteous amounts of tropical fruit, possibly breadfruit.'

On one wall are carnations and also, it has been conjectured, fuchsias, which would date the plaster ceiling to the eighteenth century.

The Cherubs of Three Cocks Lane

As you turn into Three Cocks Lane, look up, and to your left you will see an eighteenth-century carving underneath a modern canopy. From a description, which appeared in the *Gloucester Journal* in 1961, we know that it was 'the work of a well-known sculptor called Thomas Ricketts, which was erected in the portico of the Booth Hall'. The shield bears the city's coat of arms and two cherubs sit upon lions on either side.

Fan Vaulting

The fan vault is an English innovation not seen in the churches of continental Europe. It developed in the fourteenth century as a shell form that was inserted into existing Norman or Romanesque structures as an alternative to the Gothic arch. The fan vaults of Gloucester cloister were constructed from centering bays based upon earlier Norman foundations. They are one of the earliest and finest examples of English fan vaulting.

The King's Board

A structure known as the King's Board which stood in the middle of Westgate Street above Holy Trinity church was, according to tradition, given to the town by Richard II. The small size of the structure has led to the suggestion that its original function was as a preaching cross but by the 1580s it was used as a butter market. In 1693 its top was altered to accommodate a cistern for storing water pumped up from the Severn by the new water works built at Westgate Bridge. The King's Board was taken down under the Improvement Act of 1750 and re-erected in the ornamental garden of the Hyett family on the castle grounds. When the site was taken for building the new county gaol in the 1780s the King's Board was moved to the

This ceiling can be viewed in Meeks Shoe Shop in Westgate Street. The picture shows what looks like a metal flower holder containing leafy foliage.

The sculpture, by local artist Thomas Ricketts II, in Three Cocks Lane, looking rather incongruous under a modern, sixties-looking cement canopy.

The fine detail of this early English fan vaulting can be seen in the cloisters of Gloucester Cathedral.

garden of a house in Barton Street, from which it was moved by W. P. Price to the grounds of Tibberton Court in the mid-nineteenth century. In 1937 it was brought back and placed in the public gardens at Hillfield House in London Road where it remains.

Scriven's Conduit

This treasure can also be found in Hillfield Gardens. It is the remains of the head of a conduit which supplied water to the city from Mattes-Knoll, now known as Robinwoods Hill. It was originally built in 1636, from Painswick stone, for Alderman John Scriven, a local ironmonger and stood in the middle of Southgate Street almost opposite Bell Lane and to the south of the Wheat Market. Sadly, it met with the same fate as The High Cross and the King's Board being removed in 1784 in the name of progress. It was rebuilt in a garden on the site of what is now No. 24 Clarence Street. It then moved to Edgeworth Manor in Cirencester around 1830 finally returning home when it was given to the City of Gloucester and reconstructed in 1937.

The Spire

It's easy to walk by this treasure when strolling along the *via sacra* and not notice it. In St Lucy's Garden close to the grounds of Gloucester Cathedral stands the top of the spire from St John the Baptist church in Northgate Street. The top of the spire was removed in 1910 and re-erected here.

Civic Maces and Swords

The City of Gloucester still uses ancient swords in their civic ceremonies. The Mourning Sword is the older of the two swords in the council's possession, having been possibly provided under the Charter of King Richard III in 1483. The sword currently used for

The King's Board re-erected in Hillfield Gardens. Each double spandrel is a single stone crisply carved in bas-relief with a scene of Christ's ministry. The Entry into Jerusalem, the Last Supper, the Scourging of Christ, the Resurrection and the Flagellation. Effigies of heraldic beasts on the parapet and a pyramidal roof, surmounted by a cross, were taken down to make way for the cistern in 1693.

Left: Scriven's Conduit in Hillfield Gardens. Carved and moulded in a Jacobean style combining Gothic and Renaissance details. It is a small arcaded octagonal structure with eight corners which are gathered to form an open crown, capped by an elaborately carved finial which carries a statue of Jupiter Fluvius pouring rainwater on Sabrina, the goddess of the river Severn. The structure has a boldly projecting and vigorously carved lion's head at each corner and on the face of each frieze a carved medallion depicting one of the resources of the Vale of Gloucester including cider, fishing, wool and corn.

Right: The spire from the top of St John the Baptist church in Northgate Street was removed in 1910 and re-erected in St Lucy's Garden.

ceremonial purposes is the Sword of State, obtained in 1627 when an important Charter was granted to the City by King Charles I. The Sword of State is four foot and three inches long. Each of the four Maces still in use date back to 1652. They are 2 feet, 4 inches in length and made from steel with a silver gilt.

The brass Mace in Gloucester Folk Museum is the London Sergeant's Mace dated from the time of the reign of Philip and Mary (1554–1558) and is the only Sergeant's Mace of the period in existence. It was found in 1844 by workmen in Westgate Street in a house referred to as Ingram's house, the same house Bishop Hooper is thought to have spent his last night on this earth in.

Mechanical Clock

Eight generations of the Mann family have been selling jewellery on the Cross in Gloucester since 1741. Today, they can be found operating out of the iconic G. A. Baker building in Southgate Street.

Outside the premises you will see a clock made by made by Niehus Brothers of Bristol. It has five life-size automata figures striking bells on the hours and quarters, the figures standing within the arched recess on the first floor. In the centre is Father Time with an hour glass, to his right is John Bull and a Welshwoman, and to the left a Scotsman and an Irishwoman. Above the crown of the arch a decorative, cast-iron, cantilever bracket

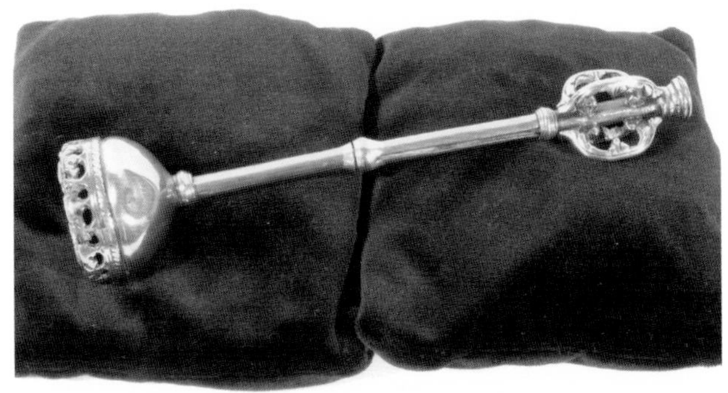

The only Sergeant's Mace of the period in existence. The legend is, it was carried by one of the guards escorting Bishop Hooper to his execution. This brass mace can be seen in Gloucester Folk Museum.

The mechanical clock, which chimes on the quarter hour, above Baker's, a jewellery shop in Southgate Street, close to The Cross.

This iconic, K6 type telephone kiosk stands in Southgate Street opposite the entrance to Gloucester Docks. The telephone is in working order and represents English design at its best.

DID YOU KNOW THAT...?

There are three Grade II-listed telephone kiosks in Gloucester. Designed in 1936 by Sir Giles Gilbert Scott and made from cast-iron, they are of the iconic type K6, square kiosk with domed roof. Situated in Southgate Street and temporarily removed from Hare Lane, they feature unperforated crowns in the top panels and margin pane glazing to the doors and windows.

supports a clock crowned by a brass finial, and hanging from the bracket is a larger bell. The bells can be heard striking on the quarter hour.

The Lucius Window

The Lucius Window is to be found in the north aisle of Gloucester Cathedral. This magnificent stained-glass window was created by John Hardman Powell, an associate of the famous architect Pugin, in 1862. He may have been the first artist in many centuries to depict King Lucius. The Gothic-style window depicts the major events in the life of the first Christian king.

Queen Anne Statue, 1665–1714

A badly weathered statue of Queen Anne stands on the south side of Spa Fields Sports Ground in Gloucester Park. It was carved from limestone in 1711 by John Ricketts I for which he received a payment of £23. Originally erected in the Spa Pleasure Ground it was moved to the garden of Paddock House in Pitt Street *c.* 1780 and from there to College Green in 1839. It has been at its present site since 1865.

Far left: This badly weathered statue of Queen Anne can be found in Gloucester Park. It is an iconic image representing the Queen in robes of state, carrying sceptre and orb, standing on a pedestal decorated with military trophies and cherubs supporting the arms of England, Ireland and Scotland.

Left: This magnificent stained glass window created by John Hardman Powell, and dedicated to King Lucius is to be found in Gloucester Cathedral.

7. Musical Gloucester

The musical heritage of Gloucester goes back to the foundation of the religious orders in the city and their tradition of chanting and composition of religious music to accompany religious services. Music is very much an integral part of the city's cultural life and extends beyond that of the church.

The Gloucestershire Group

Writing in 1919, Marion Scott wrote an article for the *Christian Science Monitor* in which she coins the phrase 'The Gloucestershire Group':

> But all these artistic movements are of common knowledge compared to what will, in future history, probably be referred to as the Gloucestershire Group...Up to the present hardly anyone has realised the interest and significance of this group, so diverse in its lines of work, so unanimous in its deep feeling for the Border country between England and Wales. Yet, in course of time, it will probably be regarded with as much admiration as the Lake Poets; perhaps even more so, for in Cumberland there were but poets alone, in Gloucester there are composers also.

John Stafford Smith, 1750–1836

John Stafford Smith was born in Gloucester and baptised in Gloucester Cathedral on 30 March 1750, the son of Martin Smith, who was the organist of Gloucester Cathedral from 1743 to 1782. He attended the King's School where he became a chorister. Like his father, he later became an organist and played at the Three Choirs Festival held at Gloucester in 1790. Stafford Smith is best known for writing the music for 'The Anacreontic Song', which became the tune for the American patriotic song 'The Star-Spangled Banner' following the war of 1812, which in 1931 was officially designated as the national anthem of the United States of America. Smith died in 1836 at the age of eighty-six, his death allegedly caused by a grape-pip lodged in his windpipe. He is buried in Gloucester Cathedral.

In 1814, Francis Scott Key wrote the poem 'Defence of Fort M'Henry' which he later re-titled, 'The Star-Spangled Banner'. The words of this poem would later be set to the music of Stafford Smith's 'Anacreon'.

Ivor Gurney, 1890–1937

> Ivor Gurney was that rare being: both poet and composer, the first Englishman to be dually-gifted in these two arts since Thomas Campion in the reign of Elizabeth I, and his output was prodigious. When he died he us left around two hundred songs, several

The music score for *Short Magnificat* in John Stafford Smith's own handwriting.

chamber and instrumental works, and over three hundred poems and verse-pieces, the best of which mark Gurney out as a creative spirit touched by genius.

Ivor gurney was born in Gloucester, the second of four children and lived at Nos 3/4 Queen Street. He was baptised at All Saints Church in Gloucester, where his cousin, Joseph Gurney, was the organist. Gurney began his schooling at the National School in Gloucester, but it was the Reverend Alfred Cheesman the curate at All Saints who encouraged Ivor to try for a choral scholarship at Gloucester Cathedral, acceptance for which would bring with it both a place in the cathedral choir and an education at the King's School. Ivor was successful, and he entered the King's School, where F. W. Harvey was already a pupil, in the autumn term of 1900. In 1906 Gurney became articled to the organist of Gloucester Cathedral, Herbert Brewer, with whom he studied music alongside two other young men, Herbert Howells and Ivor Novello, both of whom, in their very different ways, were to make a considerable impact on British music. A turning point for Gurney was reached in 1910, a year in which the Three Choirs Festival was held in Gloucester. It premiered *Fantasia on a Theme* by Thomas Tallis by Ralph Vaughan Williams and after hearing it Gurney and his friend Howells spent much of the night walking around Gloucester, talking excitedly about it. Apparently, from that moment both men were determined to become composers. During the First World War Gurney tried to enlist alongside Harvey in the 1/5th Glosters. He was rejected due to poor eyesight, but in February 1915, due to a shortage of men he was accepted as a Private in the 2/5th Glosters and subsequently in 1917 was shot in the arm. A month later he was gassed.

'Severn Meadows', one of his better known songs, written about his homesickness, was composed on the battlefields of the First World War. Returning to England he was hospitalised. This was the beginning of a lifelong battle with depression. In 1918, on 19 June, he wrote a goodbye letter to Sir Hubert Parry, then Principal of the Royal College of Music: 'I know you would rather know me dead than mad'. A month later he was transferred to the Middlesex War Hospital at Napsbury, and there he remained until his discharge from the Army in October 1918 with a pension of 12*s* per week. Back in Gloucester, Gurney faced a seemingly hopeless future, instability and depression descended into a profound mental collapse and in September 1922 Gurney was certified insane and admitted to Barnwood House mental hospital in Gloucester. Ivor Gurney died of bilateral pulmonary tuberculosis at the City of London Mental Hospital on 26 December, 1937. Five days later he was buried at Twigworth parish church.

Ivor Novello, 1893–1951

Novello was educated at the King's School in Gloucester, where he studied harmony and counterpoint with Herbert Brewer, the cathedral organist. Although Brewer had told him he would not have a career in music, Novello from his early youth showed a facility for writing songs, and when he was only fifteen, one of his songs was published. He would later say that this prolonged youthful exposure to early sacred choral music had turned his tastes, in reaction, to lush romantic music.

In 1914, at the start of the First World War, Novello was having a very different experience to his friend Ivor Gurney. He wrote 'Keep the Home Fires Burning', a song that expressed the feelings of innumerable families during the First World War. He would go on to be a composer and actor who would become one of the most popular British entertainers of the first half of the twentieth century.

Charles Hubert Hastings Parry, 1848–1918

Sir Charles Hubert Hastings Parry, 1st Baronet, was a leading English composer, teacher and historian of music. He grew up at Highnam Court, his family's country house. His interest in music was encouraged by, among others, the organist Edward Brind, at Highnam church. Brind gave Parry piano and basic harmony lessons, and took him to the Three Choirs Festival in Hereford in 1861. The experience left a great impression on Parry, and is said to have marked the beginning of his life-long association with the festival.

Following the death of his stepmother, Ethelinda Lear Gambier-Parry, in 1896, Parry succeeded to the family estate at Highnam. He was created a Knight Bachelor in 1898 and a baronet in 1902.

In the North Chantry of Gloucester Cathedral's Lady Chapel there is a commemorative stained glass window to Gurney by the artist Thomas Denny who has used fragments of fourteenth- and fifteenth-century glass in the upper sections. It uses eight lights to illustrate the different aspects of Gurney's complex personality and experience.

As a composer he is best known for the choral song 'Jerusalem', the coronation anthem 'I Was Glad', the choral and orchestral ode 'Blest Pair of Sirens', and the hymn tune 'Repton', which sets the words 'Dear Lord and Father of Mankind'. His orchestral works include five symphonies and a set of Symphonic Variations. He was head of the Royal College of Music, and concurrently professor of music at the University of Oxford from 1900 to 1908.

Charles Harford Lloyd, 1849–1919

C. H. Lloyd was an English composer and organist. He was the organist at Gloucester Cathedral from 1876 to 1881. Charles' most successful area was organ and choral but he wrote 3 clarinet pieces for his friend Randle Fynes Holme. Lloyd was founder of the Oxford University Musical Club, along with his friend Hubert Parry. A window by the renowned stained glass artist, Christopher Whall, is dedicated to Charles and is to be found in Gloucester Cathedral.

Sir Herbert Brewer, 1865–1928

Sir Alfred Herbert Brewer was an English composer and organist of Gloucester Cathedral from 1896 until his death. He was also the organist at two local churches, and also founded the city's choral society in 1905. He had been a Gloucester Cathedral chorister in his boyhood, and began his organ studies there under C. H. Lloyd. He was educated at the Cathedral School in Gloucester.

Above: The memorial tablet to Charles Hubert Hastings Parry, with an inscription by the Poet Laureate, Robert Bridges, in Gloucester Cathedral, unveiled during the Three Choirs Festival of 1922.

Left: The stained glass window dedicated to Charles Harford Lloyd in Gloucester Cathedral.

In 1913, at the Three Choirs Festival in Gloucester, Brewer was entrusted with conducting the premiere of Sibelius's tone-poem for soprano and orchestra, 'Luonnotar', Op. 70. As a composer, Brewer was fairly conservative. His output includes church music of all types, cantatas, songs, instrumental works, and orchestral music. The greater part of his life was devoted to the advancement of the standards of ecclesiastical music. Some of it has been recorded on the Priory Label. His 'Magnificat' and 'Nunc Dimittis' in D major are in the standard repertoire of Anglican Church music. An organ work, 'Marche Héroïque', is also revived from time to time and was heard at the televised 1979 funeral of Lord Mountbatten. He was knighted in 1926.

Herbert Norman Howells CH, CBE, 1892–1983

Herbert Howells was an English composer, organist, and teacher in born in Lydney, Gloucestershire. From a young age Howells was known for his musical abilities, so much so that the local squire, Charles Bathurst, arranged for him to have lessons with Herbert Brewer, organist of Gloucester Cathedral. Brewer later accepted Howells as an articled pupil which ensured a thorough grounding in keyboard playing and accompaniment, harmony and counterpoint, and composition. He was in the same class as Ivor Novello.

Howells went on to compose many works, his most poignant 'Hymnus Paradisi' a piece for soloists, chorus and orchestra in memory of his nine-year-old son, Michael, who died suddenly. It was first performed at Gloucester in 1950, conducted by the composer. Despite considerable interest in Herbert Howells' early works, it took until he was nearly sixty, with the first performance of 'Hymnus Paradisi' at the 1950 Gloucester Three Choirs Festival, for him to achieve any major success. Following this, the Festival was very keen to commission another large scale work for soloists, chorus and orchestra. Howells' response was the magnificent choral work 'Missa Sabrinensis' (Mass of the Severn). His composition 'Sine Nomine' was performed at the Three Choirs Festival.

He was also friends with Ivor Gurney, a fellow student at the Royal College of Music. A memorial to him can be found next to Gurney's grave in Twigworth Parish church.

Gloucester Choral Society

Gloucester Choral Society was founded in 1845. Herbert Howells was once its Director. Based at Gloucester Cathedral they are dedicated to presenting an interesting, varied and challenging programme of concerts each year. They rehearse in Gloucester Cathedral's historic Chapter House.

Gloucester Music Society

Founded in 1929 by Herbert Sumsion, this society promotes chamber music concerts of the highest quality. They present innovative and challenging programmes covering a wide range of music including some of the finest musicians from around the world. They perform in the beautiful and historic setting of St Mary de Lode church, which has a superb acoustic.

The City of Gloucester Mummers

Mummers' Plays have been performed for hundreds of years. They are folk dramas

DID YOU KNOW THAT...?

In 1724, the cathedrals of Gloucester, Worcester and Hereford established The Three Choirs Festival making it one of the oldest classical choral music festivals in the world.

based on the legend of St George and the Seven Champions of Christendom. They were originally mime or dumb shows, the word 'mummers' originating from the Middle English word 'mum', meaning silent. Hence the phrase 'keeping mum'.

The City of Gloucester Mummers started life in the back room of the Ship Inn on The Quay, in August 1969. Their first performance was at the Ship Inn Folk Club on Christmas Eve 1969 and two days later on Boxing Day they performed outside the Cathedral and have done so every Boxing Day since, singing the traditional Gloucester City Wassail.

1970 saw the first City of Gloucester St George's Day celebrations. They performed The Gloucester Mumming Play, in existence since the 1880s. The tradition of presenting the Mayor of Gloucester with a rose on St George's Day has continued ever since.

Above: The City of Gloucester Mummers performing on Boxing Day outside Gloucester Cathedral.

Left: The stained glass window, dedicated to Herbert Brewer, by the renowned stained glass artist, Veronica Whall, who was the daughter of Christopher Whall, in Gloucester Cathedral.

8. Epicurean Gloucester

Since medieval times, Gloucester has been famous for, and associated with, food which hails from the region.

Cheese

Smart's Farm, Gloucester are a family farm making traditional, handmade Gloucester Cheese and is one of only four traditional single Gloucester producers in the world. Their herd of sixty-six cows includes the ancient breed of Gloucester Cattle. A rare cheese which originated on Gloucestershire farms over 200 years ago, it was originally eaten at home, while the harder Double Gloucester was sent away to provide the farmer's income. Single Gloucester is made from full cream milk from the morning milking and skimmed milk from the evening milking and is aged for at least three weeks. It is described as having a deliciously light texture and beautifully balanced taste, with a cool, clean tang and grassy sub-flavours. Whereas Double Gloucester is made from full cream milk from both the morning and evening milkings, with added annatto, a traditional natural dye and then aged for a minimum of six months. It is described as having a rich, mellow, powerful, earthy, almost smoky taste.

Cheese Rolling

Cheese Rolling is an ancient Gloucester custom which today attracts competitors from around the world. The first written evidence of Cheese Rolling on Coopers Hill was found in a message to the Gloucester Town Crier in 1826 although it is believed to have been in existence way before that. It involves chasing a 7.5lb Double Gloucester Cheese down a precipitous hill in death defying tradition. At top speed, the cheese is estimated to reach 70 mph, taking approximately 12 seconds to get from the top to the bottom of Cooper's Hill. Local cheesemakers, Smart's Farm, have traditionally provided the Double Gloucester Cheese wheel, weighing 7.5lb (3 kg) to the famous Cheese Rolling competition held in May on Cooper's Hill.

DID YOU KNOW THAT...?

Many farmhouses can still be seen today with their louvered tallets, which is where the cheese was stored before being sold to the cheese factors. These factors would walk on the cheese to check that they weren't 'hoven' or too soft.

Gloucester Old Spot

The Gloucester Old Spot is said to be the largest pig ever to be bred. They graze in apple orchards, clearing up the windfalls, earning the nickname the Orchard Pig. Its white coat has large, clearly defined black spots giving rise to the legend that the black spots were bruises from falling apples. They became the first breed of any species in the world to be accorded Traditional Speciality Guaranteed status by the EU Commission putting it on a par with Champagne and Parma ham.

Lampreys

Since medieval times lampreys have been a great delicacy in Gloucester. The Lamprey is a very ancient and primitive group of jawless vertebrates. Their common name, lamprey, is probably derived from the Latin *lampetra*, to mean stone licker. Most species of lamprey are parasites and have long, eel-like bodies that lack scales. They use their jawless mouths to attach to a host fish by suction before sucking out the living tissues. Unlike other fish, the lamprey has no scales, jaws, gill covers or bony skeleton. Fossil evidence has shown lampreys date from before the dinosaurs.

The Lamprey Pie consists of baked Lamprey, set in cool syrup and covered with a large raised crust. When the crust is opened, the liquid is mixed with wine and spices, and then spooned onto slices of white bread in a dish warmed over a chafer or hotplate. The lamprey is then cut into 'gobbets as thin as a groat' and placed on top of the bread and sauce. Here is an old recipe for Lamprey Pie:

> Take your Lamprey and gut him, and take away the black string in the back, wash him very well, and dry him, and season him with nutmeg, pepper and salt, then lay him into

Above: This 1834 painting of a Gloucester Old Spot, by John Miles, is an example of 'naïve art'.

Left: Chris Anderson, a Brockworth local and a regular winner of the annual Cheese Rolling competition held on Cooper's Hill, preparing himself for his race.

your pie in pieces with butter in the bottom, and some shelots and bay leaves and more butter, so close it and bake it, and fill it up with melted butter, and keep it cold, and serve it in with some mustard and sugar.

DID YOU KNOW THAT...?

Henry I of England is said to have died in 1135 from eating a surfeit of lampreys of which he was excessively fond. Samuel Pepys mentioned them in his diaries and spoke of how they were a great favourite of medieval epicures. In 1952 Howard Sibson, who was then Gloucester's Sheriff, reintroduced the age-old local custom of sending a decorated lamprey pie to each newly-crowned monarch. Thanks to Mr Sibson, such a pie was prepared for the coronation of the present Queen in 1953. She received another for her Silver Jubilee and a third for the Golden Jubilee.

Most royal families of England were particularly fond of lampreys, as it was considered a delicacy at the English Court. The tradition was for the people of Gloucester to present the monarch with a lamprey pie every Christmas. In 1530 the prior of Llanthony Secunda in Gloucester sent cheise carp and baked lampreys to Henry VIII at Windsor. It was also customary at the commencement of the fishing season to send the sovereign the first lamprey caught in the river. The intermittent custom of the city of Gloucester to present the sovereign at Christmas with a lamprey pie with a raised crust may have originated in the time of Henry I of England, who was inordinately fond of lamprey and who frequently held his court at Gloucester during the Christmas season.

Elvers

Elvers are young eels, beginning their life as eel larvae, they drift from their birthplace in the Sargasso Sea for three years across the Atlantic Ocean, a distance of 2,000 miles to finally end up in the Severn Estuary. Elvers are fished on the spring tides, at night, using a specially shaped elver net.

Traditionally, fishermen consumed elvers as a cheap dish and as such a traditional method of cooking elvers developed in Gloucester. First scold them in hot water, then fry some bacon in a pan, remove the bacon and fry the elvers for a minute then crack an egg into the pan and cook. They taste like fishy spaghetti!

Gloucester Cattle

Gloucester Cattle are one of the oldest dairy breeds in Britain and date back to the thirteenth century. Gloucester's were used as draught oxen and for small scale production of milk and cheese, traditionally used for making Single and Double Gloucester Cheese. They are distinctive looking with short horns, a black-brown body, white belly and black head and legs with a white stripe, which runs along the back.

DID YOU KNOW THAT...?

William Hunt's short book *The Victorian Elver Wars* recalls the ban on elvering along the lower Severn in the year 1874. It was imposed by the Severn Fisheries Board and immediately brought unexpected resistance. The Gloucester judiciary, politicians and locals got involved culminating in June 1876 in a three day inquiry which was held at Gloucester to look into the 'elver question'. A subsequent report recommending lifting the ban was produced but it would be as late as July 1876 before agreement was finally reached, and conditional elvering was once more permitted. It was probably the first recorded attempt at elver conservation.

About the Author

Christine Jordan lives in Gloucestershire. She is the author of *City of Secrets*, her debut historical fiction novel, set in medieval Gloucester. You can find out more about Christine's writing from her website, christinejordan.co.uk.

Opposite left: This stupendous lamprey pie was baked for Her Majesty Queen Elizabeth II in 1953 in her coronation year. The pie weighed forty-two pounds, was eighteen inches high and fourteen inches in diameter. Apart from the cushion under the Royal Crown, the whole of the pie was edible, and all the embellishments, including the Royal Coat of Arms and the Coat of Arms of the City of Gloucester, were in colour.

Opposite right: Elver fishing on the River Severn still goes on today using the traditional elver nets.

Opposite below: Distinctive-looking Gloucester cattle. They were almost extinct in the 1970s until a local farmer, Charles Martell, rescued them and has created a thriving herd at his farm in Dymock. At the time there were only sixty-eight of these cattle left in the world.

Acknowledgements

A huge thank-you goes to David Rice from Gloucester's City Museum who was immensely helpful in checking and providing sources for my research and to Jill Evans for reading the first draft whilst wearing her editor's hat.

The primary sources for the research of this book were:

Counsell, George Worral: *The History and Description of the City Of Gloucester*
Fosbrooke, Thomas Dudley: *An Original History of the city of Gloucester*
Fullbrook-Leggatt, L.E.W.O.: *Anglo-Saxon and Medieval Gloucester*
Fullbrook-Leggatt, L.E.W.O.: *Roman Gloucester (*GLEVUM*)*
Rudder, Samuel: *A New History of Gloucestershire*
Rudge, Thomas: *The History and Antiquities of Gloucester*
Stevenson, William Henry: *Rental of All the Houses in Gloucester, AD 1455. From a Roll in the Possession of the Corporation of Gloucester. Compiled by R. Cole* ... Edited, with a Translation by W. H. Stevenson
British History Online
British Listed Buildings Online
GADARG
GSIA
Grace's Guide
GRO

Huge thanks to all those who gave me their permission to use their images:

Gloucester Museums Service Art Collection
Wendy Harris
Roger Smith
Lorraine Hopkins
Mark Wheaver
Churchcrawler (Phil)
Peter Clarkson
David Ward
John Williams